99

Voices of
CHILDREN of DIVORCE

Voices of
CHILDREN of DIVORCE

Dr. David Royko

Golden Books

NEW YORK

888 Seventh Avenue
New York, NY 10106

Designed by Gwen Petruska Gürkan

Manufactured in the United States of America

10 9 8 7 6 5 4 3 2 1

Library of Congress Cataloging-in-Publication Data

Royko, David.
    Voices of children of divorce / David Royko.
        p.   cm.
    Includes bibliographical references.
    ISBN 1-58238-006-6 (hc : alk. paper)
    1. Children of divorced parents—United States—Case studies.
    2. Divorce—United States—Case studies.   3. Parent and child—
    United States—Case studies.   I. Title.
    HQ777.5.R69   1999
    306.89—dc21   98-24696
                                                          CIP

To my late parents,
Mike Royko and Carol Joyce (Duckman) Royko,
who put up with me as I grew up; to my wife, Karen Miller Royko,
who sometimes wonders if I ever did grow up;
and to my boys, Jake and Ben, who I hope will put up with me
as I try to help them grow up.

Contents

CONTENTS

Introduction

For the past ten years I have worked as a mediator at the Circuit Court of Cook County's Marriage and Family Counseling Service (MFCS) in Chicago, trying to help divorcing parents resolve custody and visitation disputes.

Typically, divorce mediation is handled by a private mediator, and the couples decide for themselves to try mediation. There may be a dispute about the house, about money, or even about the children, but they agree on one thing: They would like to resolve their differences and avoid dragging everyone through a trial.

At MFCS it can be a very different story. The Circuit Court of Cook County is the largest unified court system in the United States; its mediation department of twenty-one psychologists, social workers, and attorneys is among the largest of its type in the country. The parents we see are *ordered* by a judge to attend mediation, often against their will. We do not mediate any financial or property disputes—those conflicts are for the private mediators to hash out. Instead, we handle only the most volatile of feuds: custody and visitation.

The psychological and emotional torment of these cases makes most other divorces look courteous. It is no coincidence that the only Cook County judge murdered while sitting on the bench was not a criminal court judge or a civil court judge but a divorce judge. Few events can drive an otherwise sane person mad like divorce, and no divorce cases are as brutal as those in which the parents are fighting over the children.

Since many of our clients are the victims of physical or emotional abuse by their spouses, we must ensure that the mediation process provides a safe and effective environment and does not become another circumstance for abuse. Therefore, we use a variety of techniques to help parents resolve their custody disputes: standard mediation, where two parents are together with one mediator; co-mediation, where two mediators meet with the parents together; caucusing, where the parents meet together but with short breaks to allow the mediator to meet individually with each parent in order to overcome specific obstacles; and, finally, shuttle mediation, a somewhat cumbersome process in which there is no face-to-face contact between the parents—each parent is seen separately by the mediator, then waits in a protected area while the other parent is seen, alternating in this way for the duration of each session.

Often these parents do not want resolution, they want retribution and revenge. They want their day in court. They want the world to know what they or their children have suffered at the hands of their tormentors, their spouses. *These* are the parents we see in the mediation department—and their children are the reason our department exists.

* * *

It would be nice to say that I ended up working with children of divorce because it was my lifelong calling, but the truth is I had just put a bid on a house and needed more money. I reluctantly left a job in a hospital that I enjoyed and accepted the position at MCFS because it paid more. Though the work sounded intriguing, all told it was not an auspicious beginning—and I did not feel any better once I started. First, there were the angry couples—enough alone to give me second thoughts. Second, I was now part of the court system. Even though my experience with the court system did not extend beyond traffic court or jury duty, the thought of courtrooms made me uncomfortable if not downright fearful. Somehow, even though we are all innocent until proven guilty, I've always found it hard to feel anything but guilty while looking up at a judge looking down at me. Almost instantly I found myself wondering how such a setting must feel to the children stuck in the system. These children were among my new clients—and it was with them that I first began to see the rewards of my new job.

Over the past ten years at MFCS I have interviewed well over one thousand of these children. My time with them has provided some of the most meaningful hours I have had in my professional life. These children are frequently eloquent, poignant, and enlightening about divorce—from the six-year-old who begged me to let her move in with me to get away from her mother's constant criticism of her father, to the teenager who told me that he wished he were gay so he would never be tempted to get married and have children to "screw up." In turns heartbreaking, perceptive, funny, frustrating, startling, touching, horrifying, and everything else imaginable, their stories are best at expressing what divorce is like for those caught in the middle.

As part of our mediation service we interview children between the ages of four and eighteen, not to put them in the position of having to make decisions for their parents—in fact, the whole point of the mediation process is to prevent them from getting caught in the middle—but rather to get a sense of how they are doing under the circumstances. By definition, if we see them, that means Mom and Dad are fighting over them, and the children will usually be under a tremendous amount of stress. Our meeting with the children is a chance for us to say "time out" and to determine exactly what they need, be it counseling, therapy, or simply an opportunity to express what their parents' conflict is doing to them.

Divorcing parents often lose sight of the injuries suffered by their children. During a divorce, parents have the luxury of being able to take a one-sided view of things. They may no longer see, or wish to see, anything that might be positive in the other parent. But most often children remain devoted, if only in secret, to both sides. Their love for Mom and Dad has not changed, though now it is overlaid with a mist of fear and uncertainty. While it once was fine to say, "I love you, Dad," with Mom in the room, now it may not be. The child's internal tug-of-war has begun.

Even the most dedicated parents might not see how deeply their children suffer. Sometimes this is because their children become experts at hiding their emotions, but more often it is because the parents wish to believe that their children are being spared the pain of divorce. While it is commonly accepted that divorce can have a significant impact on children, parents rarely think that the children who are hurt or damaged are their *own*. "Thank God my kids are doing okay," they think. "At least they're not going through what my cousin's kids went through." When I discuss with parents the conversations I have had with their children, they are often shocked by what I report. They are also moved—at times to such a degree that they drop their fight and begin to move on.

* * *

No child emerges from divorce unaffected, but how parents deal with their children—and each other—during a divorce will determine just how deep and visible any scars will be. To that end, for parents who are separating, are already separated, or are in the process of divorcing, here are some guidelines to help their children through this tough time. The rules emphasize the concept of co-parenting, which involves the continued cooperation between parents who otherwise may have nothing to do with each other.

1. Keep children from being caught in the middle. Parents should communicate directly with each other. Avoid using the children as "messengers" or putting them in the position of having to "choose" one parent over the other. That way, each parent-child relationship can remain separate and secure.

2. If you as a parent do not have something nice to say about the other parent, then do not say anything at all. Other-

wise, the child will feel a need to either express his loyalty to you or defend the other parent. In both cases, the child loses.

3. Parent-child time is sacred and needs to be respected by each parent—not as a favor for the other parent but as a gift to the child, one that he or she deserves and needs.

4. Honor your commitments to your children, especially in the area of time spent together. For noncustodial parents, this means being on time for pickups, avoiding cancellations, and making sure the time together is focused on the child. Children often feel abandoned during a divorce and wonder if a parent can divorce them as well. Being consistent with visitation tells children that they can count on you to be there for them. For custodial parents it is important to set aside time for the children for the same reasons. They may need more comforting and assurance during and after the divorce.

5. New and appropriate boundaries must be created. First, each parent must accept the other parent's role in the child's life and not use the parent-child bond to trespass into the other parent's personal life. For example, a child should not be expected to retrieve items that one parent wants from the other parent's residence or be asked to spy or report on the activities of the other parent, such as who he or she is dating. Second, the boundary between parent and child must be firmly set. If a child asks why the divorce is happening, a parent must walk a fine line between suitable information and total honesty. What one might tell a close friend—"I could take all the bickering and money problems we had, but when he started sleeping with his carpool partner, that did it"—could be confusing or even devastating to a child.

6. Maintaining the hierarchy of the parent-child relationship is critical. Do not look to the child for comfort and support. Children are often eager to step into the void and take care of Mom or Dad. This is unfair to the child and can impede the child's own process of healing.

These guidelines are important to help the child keep from feeling that he or she has slipped through the cracks during divorce. However, there are situations where co-parenting is neither desirable nor safe. If there is a history of abusive behavior, measures must be taken to safeguard, as much as possible, against any future instances of abuse. Children do best when their environment is one of safety and respect, and it is the responsibility of the parents to create such an environment. If family violence is a concern, aid should be sought through a local shelter, hospital, hotline, clergy, or mental health professional experienced in the area of family violence.

*   *   *

Some of the comments made by the children in this book may be a bit jolting, and none more so than this one from Natalie, nineteen: "Sometimes, I honestly wish my dad had died [instead of getting a divorce]. . . . People would have sympathy for us. People would have understood. They wouldn't have judged." As sad as that may be, it illustrates the parallel between the two major categories of loss for a child: death and divorce. Children often describe being more terrified of divorce than of parental death. Yet, as Natalie suggests, a child whose parents have died stands a better chance of getting the attention he or she needs than does a child whose parents have split up. From an adult's perspective it is easy to underestimate the weight of a child's grief when his parents divorce.

Like anyone who has experienced a major loss, children of divorce must be allowed to grieve the loss. Stages of grieving that children undergo during divorce include anger, denial, bargaining, depression, and, it is hoped, acceptance, stages that are typically associated with death and dying but can also apply to anyone experiencing a severe loss. It can be difficult with children, however, to recognize these stages for what they are, since a particular stage of grieving can look one way in an adult but completely different in a child. An understanding of these stages can aid parents or other adults in helping a child heal.

It is important to realize that the stages of grieving are not as clear-cut in real life as they are on paper. How long the child grieves and at what points during a divorce a child may go through certain stages are dependent on many factors, from the child's psychological and emotional state, and personality, to how the parents are coping with the divorce themselves and whether the parent seeks help, if necessary, for the child. Also, these stages can overlap. Certain stages might last longer than others, and a child might backtrack to an earlier stage of grieving, especially during times of increased stress. Still, it helps to have a general idea of what to expect from a child who is working through his grief.

Anger is among the easiest of these stages to spot and understand. A younger child who is having more tantrums or has started biting and an older child who seems to be flying off the handle for no apparent reason might be expressing anger in the only way they know how, especially if they are not being encouraged to share their feelings verbally. A teen who becomes abusive to younger siblings might be venting anger that he is actually feeling toward his parents.

Denial is a powerful defense that allows the child to digest the magnitude of a loss at her own pace, and it is a signal that the loss is simply too much for the child to take in at the moment. However, denial in children can often lull parents into the false belief that everything is fine. "She's so resilient, she never even gave a second thought to the divorce after we told her about it." But no child goes through her parents' divorce without experiencing pain. Children simply don't know how to cope with such feelings—or to express them—and will choose "denial" as a way to try to make such feelings go away. Parents who believe their child has adjusted perfectly have probably missed small signals of distress that the child is probably sending out. A child might tell her school friends that everything is fine at home even after one parent has moved out. She might tell herself that the situation is temporary or that it is just a bad dream from which she will someday awaken. Though denial is a valuable defense, it is time-limited. Eventually, reality can no longer be ignored, even by the most sturdy of children. A child may be able to handle pain with denial for a little while, but at some point that pain must be faced.

The phenomenon of "bargaining" might be less obvious. For example, a parent who is trying to keep the marriage together may openly bargain with a spouse, saying, "I'll change if you stay," where a child may bargain more covertly. For instance, a child whose room is usually in a state of disarray may begin keeping his room in perfect order, making his bed every day and neatly folding and putting away his clothes. In that child's mind, his room might have caused Mom and Dad's arguing. Therefore, if he keeps things neat, Mom and Dad won't need to argue and won't divorce.

Younger children are especially prone to such thinking, since they believe that the universe revolves around them. By that thinking, however, they also bear the ultimate responsibility, which is one reason that they often take divorce so hard, since they consider themselves to blame when they "fail" to prevent it. Bargaining, in all its varied forms, is a child's attempt to correct what she believes she caused in the first place.

Depression is another condition that can be difficult to recognize in a child. Often the result of anger that is repressed, depression in a child may be obvious from certain signs such as lethargy, loss of appetite, disturbances of sleep, and feelings of hopelessness and despair, but it can also show up as a mix of despair and anger. Fights in school, heightened trouble with siblings, an increased oppositional stance toward authority—all can be symptoms of depression in children. Where an adult might verbalize his or her pain, the child may "act out" these feelings.

One excellent way to help children with depression is to find a local support group that specializes in divorce or loss. One of the best known is the nonprofit organization Rainbows, but there are many to choose from around the country. To locate such groups in your area, try contacting your local schools, places of worship, or public libraries.

These support groups allow children to realize that what they have gone through is not unique, that what they feel is okay, that they are not weird because of these feelings and experiences, and that they are not alone. Even though divorce is a statistically common experience for children, the destruction of one's family can severely disrupt a child's sense of fitting in with peers. Support groups can help children regain a sense of themselves within their peer groups while working through the grieving process.

It also doesn't hurt if parents join similar groups for adults. There is an old saying that many therapists like to use, "A child can never be mentally healthier than his parents," but in my experience, parents tend to be open to the idea of seeking help for their children but will often balk at the suggestion that they themselves get into some form of support group, counseling, or therapy. "I don't have the time" is the most common retort. While time may be at a premium, the need for support is critical during this phase of their lives. To use an analogy, anyone who has flown on a commercial airline has heard the safety speech given prior to takeoff: "In the event of a loss in air pressure, make sure your own oxygen mask is secure before attending to your child's." In other words, as paradoxical as it may seem, parents must think of themselves first in order to best take care of the needs of the children. A parent who is an emotional mess or who is exhausted from trying to hold it all together is much less helpful than one who is getting help while grappling with divorce. In this case, what is good for the parent is good for the child.

*   *   *

Over a three-year period I spoke with scores of children for this book. Their ages ranged from five to twenty-one. Their parents had either been divorced for years, were in the process of divorcing, or even, in a couple of cases, had yet to separate. They came from all over the United States, with the majority calling the Midwest their home; they ran the full spectrum socioeconomically from impoverished to affluent; and they represent many races and religions. All were seen voluntarily for the express purpose of writing this book. All of the names of the children and their families, friends, and acquaintances have been changed to protect their identities. Many place names and locations have been changed as well.

I went as high as age twenty-one because, even though an eighteen-year-old is considered in many ways to be an adult, when it comes to parents, we are often children until much later. In fact, when parents divorce, it is the child in his or her late teens or early twenties who tends to be overlooked by parents, friends, relatives, and society in general. Because children are usually becoming independent at that age, parents often assume that they will not be affected by the event as much as younger children. Indeed, parents will often wait until their children are in their late teens or in college before divorcing, precisely for this reason. Older children may have a different perspective on and reaction to a divorce, but they are still deeply affected by it.

Throughout this book I use the term "divorce" because the experience of "divorce" is still the most common for children whose parents have split up, whether or not they were ever married. The fact of marriage has little or no bearing on a child's experience when parents break up. Likewise, even if parents remain married for many years after separating, the experience of the separation is usually indistinguishable from a legal divorce from the vantage point of the child.

Finally, I have not included interviews from my work for the court because those families were being seen by me for the purpose of court-ordered mediation, not for a book.

The fact is, despite being at the center of a custody dispute, most of the children I interview in mediation are just like other kids who are going through their parents' divorce. The horror stories of divorce—a twelve-year-old driven to drugs, a thirteen-year-old to armed robbery, or a fourteen-year-old to suicide—are not the norm. The damage that comes from divorce is often invisible, at least while the child is still a child. Therefore, like most of the kids I see in mediation, virtually all the children I interviewed for this book are what you might call "normal" or "ordinary" children. As a group they are probably no different from most kids you know. And what I have come to find is that these "ordinary" children have some extraordinary things to say about divorce, as might the children you know if they were given the chance to be heard.

*   *   *

Because children are often extremely hesitant to share with their parents their feelings about divorce, even if the relationship is a good one, the words in this book, spoken by other children, can help parents understand what might be hiding behind the words of their own children. It is not necessary to find quotes or passages that match precisely what your own child might be thinking. It is enough to know that your own child has plenty going on inside.

This material can be used as a springboard to open up lines of communication between adults and children. While much of this material expresses what many children feel and think, any individual child will, of course, have his or her own unique perspective. As such, she should be allowed to express those opinions and speak with someone with whom she feels comfortable, whether a parent, a support group, or simply an adult friend.

I also hope that adult children of divorce will find this book helpful. Sadly, it has been only in the last twenty years or so that divorce has become a topic open for discussion, which means that many adults who suffered silently through divorce as children or who expressed their pain in indirect and destructive ways are still carrying a weight that this book might help lighten.

Ultimately I want this book to help divorcing parents better understand what their children are going through so they can take steps to care for them the best way they can. In so doing, parents can make life easier for their children as they go through this difficult time, thus increasing the chances that their children will grow into an adulthood that includes healthy and satisfying love relationships of their own.

One

BEFORE THE DIVORCE: The Way We Were

*Sometimes children are aware of an approaching divorce before
their parents are, while other children are taken completely by
surprise. We begin by hearing what the children had to say
about their home life when everybody lived under the same
roof, for better and for worse.*

Robin, 19 My dad slept in a sleeping bag on the living room floor
downstairs for as long as I can remember. It's funny, 'cause I never
thought that it was weird, ever. When I was little, I used to get up and
go downstairs really early. He went to work at seven in the morning, so
it was when he was still in bed. I used to go down and I'd lay with him,
and then he'd get up, and then I'd get up and go back to my bed.

I never thought it was weird at all. It was like, "I'm going to go sleep
with Dad in the sleeping bag." It was always that way, as far back as I
can remember. I was talking to Dad about it a while ago, and he said
that for something like seven years he slept on the floor downstairs. It's
like, "I never remember you sleeping upstairs." I remember my parents
sleeping in the same bed once. My sister and I made them breakfast, so
it must have been some special day.

Things that I thought were normal, I grew up and then discovered
that they were not normal at all. It never crossed my mind until years
later when I was thinking, "You know, I never remember Dad sleeping
upstairs, only one night, like one morning." That's weird. That makes
me angry. I was mad at myself for a long time about it, but now I'm just

like, "Well, that's stupid because how would I know it wasn't normal?" I'm dumber than a rock, but if you don't know, you don't know.

Jewel, 18 Once I woke up in the middle of the night. Fortunately my brother was still asleep, and I guess that was the first time I ever knew that anything was wrong with my parents. My dad said to my mom, "I have not loved you in twenty years." I was twelve, and so I was just like, "So my dad didn't love my mom when I was created." That alone repeats over and over in my head every time I see him. Every time I see him.

Jamal, 20 Oh, I remember every aspect about this divorce, every aspect about my parents' lives. I have a great memory, but for some reason the divorce sticks out in my mind more than even my college basketball career. I can't remember what I did in a game, what happened four, five, or six months ago. But I can remember what was said, when it happened, how it happened, what day it was.

Arnie, 13 The arguments were hard to listen to in the evening time or morning time. In the daytime they were just skirmishes, nighttime they were full-blown wars. Yell, yell, yell, yell, yell. About bills, financial disagreements, taxes, all that lovely stuff.

Darnell, 14 When I was nine, I couldn't enjoy my birthday. My mom, her girlfriend's sister and brother, and two of my friends went to Show Biz Pizza. What I did was, I just sat there in fear, 'cause I knew my mom wasn't supposed to be out this late, because she wasn't supposed to spend money on my birthday. When we got home, sure enough there they went, and I was scared. That was the end part of their marriage.

Loretta, 21 I remember when I was really little that they did love each other, because I remember them goofing around with me. When I was three and four, we had this thing called sandwich hugs, and they would pick me up and hold me up between them while they were hugging, without using any hands, because they just squashed together. But that stopped quite a while ago. I don't remember them really being in love or anything.

Christina, 19 They hadn't discussed what marriage meant to them before they got married, and part of it was that Mom was pregnant, so they hadn't talked about it. I guess that they both had had an open relationship, open to seeing other people, and that was something that drove them apart. It wasn't something that my mom wanted, but he wanted it. Originally, they said they would have equal parts in the family. Then after the first year, he said, "I'm gonna go to work now, and you're going to sit at home with the kids," and so he talked his way out of it.

Tom, 12 My grandparents have been notorious for divorce. Almost all of them have been remarried. Only one grandparent out of all my grandparents wasn't, and the one that didn't get remarried said, "I was dumped." She says it didn't bother her.

Wendy, 17 My father grew up in a house where what his parents did was, sort of like my parents, as soon as they figured out that they had a problem, they got divorced. It's sort of as if the kid's going to have an operation, you want him to have it at three or four, because then she won't really remember it. I don't know that this is what they were thinking at the time, but this is the way I think of it. If you get divorced, you may as well do it when the kid's really young.

Jewel, 18 My dad lived eight hundred miles away, in Maryland, from the time I was nine, when my parents were still married, until I was twelve, because he quit his law firm in town and decided to get a job at a bank in Maryland. And he carried on with this woman from the time I was nine until I was thirteen. And now he's still carrying on with this woman. We'd go out to visit him, and we'd stay in her condo, and he would tell us every time, "This is my friend's condo," and so I'm thinking, "Friend from work. It's a guy."

Well, we would go there, and she would answer the door, and I was like, "Okay, this is your friend?" And at first he was like, "Oh, this is his wife, and he's out of town. She'll stay upstairs, and we'll stay downstairs, and everything will be fine." I'm like, "Okay, whatever." He didn't stay downstairs anyway.

And then her children came in, and they were in their twenties. I heard them talking one night, and I came to find out their dad had been dead for four years. But I still trusted my father. The boundary hadn't been broken because my parents were so good at keeping their problems out of my sight. My brother and I had no idea.

Then I went home, and I said, "Mom, this lady's really nice. She does stuff with us," and my mom was like, "Oh, that's good." But she was noticeably upset, and she was like, "I'll have to write her a thank-you note." Then my mom started mentioning the word "divorce," and then I went to school one day, and everybody at school was like, "I'm sorry about your parents," and I said, "What?" And they were like, "Well, they got a divorce, right?" And I said, "No."

I went home that night, and my father had come home from Maryland. At the dinner table he said, "Should we tell them now?" and I was in mid-bite. My mom said, "No, that's kind of inappropriate for the dinner table." So my brother and I stopped eating, and we kind of just sat there. Finally, we left the dinner table and went to the living room. My brother and I were both sitting with my mom. My dad goes, "We're getting a divorce," and we just sat there crying and hugging my mom. Then we went upstairs, and my dad left.

Then the same night he came back completely drunk and demanded that we come out, to go with him. I guess if I was in the situation where I had been sleeping with somebody else for an extended period of time, it would still hurt me to see my children siding with the person that I'm no longer in love with. That would hurt me. And I'm sure that he was terribly upset, because I do kind of think that he might have a soul somewhere. I figure he was kind of upset and drowned his sorrows, thinking that if he took us away, we'd love him again.

Michelle, 14 I remember them arguing a lot. All the time. I mean, I never saw them express any emotional tenderness toward each other, but, then, my mom's not that kind of person.

Martin, 18 We were at the dinner table, and they said they had a real big thing to tell us. We thought it was Disney World or something, and we were like, "Oh, yeah! All right!" We were all excited.

But then it was basically "We're not happy living together anymore, so we are gonna get divorced." We didn't understand why. I mean, I didn't understand the emotional level. I wasn't a wreck over it. I wasn't upset. I was most concerned with who got the big-screen TV. I actually started packing that night even though the divorce wasn't until the end of that school year. I kind of took it in stride: "Oh, okay. No big deal." Because we'd moved on the average of once every year anyway. And, also, a lot of my friends' parents were divorced. Actually, my best friend at the time. So it was like, "This happens to my friends, too."

Patty, 16 They got divorced when I was ten, but they separated when I was nine. It sucked. I had no idea it was coming. I probably should have, thinking back. It was really bad, but if it's all you've ever seen, I think you pretty much accept it. You don't know that it's not a normal situation. I never really thought about it. Like, I knew that it sucked, but I didn't think, "Hey, this is really bad," you know? I was with friends one day—I was maybe twelve—and I was like, "Your parents are really nice to each other. That's so amazing. Boy, that's so cool." And they're just like, "Whatever, man."

When a parent is blinded by anger toward the other parent, he or she can forget that the child is also in the line of fire, as Nicole's experience reveals.

Nicole, 19 My mom had picked me up from school. We went to the bank because Mom and Dad had to cash a check and split it half and half. I was chatting with my dad when Mom gave him the money, and she just gave him the extra change. "Here, take it, don't worry about it."

Well, he thought that she was being conniving or something, and he didn't like that at all. He was like, "Oh, you think I need the change?"

He threw the money at her and ended up hitting me with change, and I was just like, "Why?" He pulled out of the bank parking lot, and he pulled up and tried to hit her with the car and just missed her and ended up going on the sidewalk, like six inches from the bank, and then pulling away, just screeching away. I just thought, "He just tried to run over my mom and me." I don't know if he would have actually hit us, but he was certainly trying to scare us. And I thought, "Why does he do that when he knows I'm here? Does he not care that I'm his kid?" It seemed like he was letting their problems get in the way of his relationship with us, and that was the hardest thing in the world to take, seeing that his relationship with us didn't stop him from being bitter or hard on her.

Ken, 13 I found out that they were probably getting divorced partially by them telling me and partially by figuring it out myself. By the time they partially told me, I could just tell by the fights and stuff, and I kinda figured out that most likely they were getting divorced. Because, you know, they'd been going to court and stuff, getting all these papers and all that stuff. So I put two and two together. It's kind of easy, you know. It's just common sense.

Carie, 15 They never fought much at all. I think they fought more the year after they told us. I never heard them fight, ever. But I don't remember my parents ever being real affectionate, either.

Then one night, it was a family meeting. We had pizza, and then they cleared the table. I don't really remember exactly how they said it, but my older brother started crying. Then my younger brother, he was in kindergarten, he went back to watching a movie because he didn't understand what they were saying. We thought he was selfish for going back and watching TV.

But I didn't know that it was coming. When they told us, I ran upstairs to see if it wasn't just a dream and I was still asleep. Then they kept us home that night from a party at school. My brothers and I all wanted to go, but it was a family meeting night.

Then came the tension. They started telling other people they were divorcing, putting it down on paper that they were getting a divorce. Then you could definitely tell there was tension. Sometimes they wouldn't talk to each other. They seemed to disagree with each other more.

For some odd reason I just didn't care about the whole thing. My mom was still the person who did everything. She went to all the stuff, she talked to all the parents. My dad's the kind of person who didn't participate much. When they went to functions, it's not like they sat at opposite ends of the room. They still sat next to each other. It didn't show a difference for a long time, till we moved.

But everyone was saying, "Oh, are your parents divorced? Well, how come they're still living together?" The girls at school got really sappy and stuff. But then everyone started getting really rude and bitchy to each other, so I was ready to move, ready for new friends.

Barb, 18 There was a lot of screaming—or, I mean, well, my dad doesn't scream, but he was speaking in very forceful Chinese, and my mom in hysterical Chinese, very loud, yelling—and there was a lot of stuff that I couldn't understand, but I knew it was just angry. I guess it's kind of good in a way that I didn't understand what they were saying. Maybe it wasn't as wounding. I wouldn't hear some insults. Or I wouldn't hear what the issues were that they were arguing so strongly about. I really had no idea. I just tried to close my ears and not hear it anymore, because it was hurting my head and I wanted it to be quiet. Like all children when their parents fight, I wanted to be the heroic one who comes out and says, "Stop this! If you love me, if you love my brother, stop it!" But I never did.

Jewel, 18 When I was growing up, school would start at seven. I'd get up at six, my dad would be asleep until eight that morning, so I'd never see my dad in the morning. I'd come home, I'd eat dinner, and very rarely would he be there for dinner. He'd always be at the office doing whatever. So I would go to bed, and my dad would come home later. My dad was an alcoholic, so a lot of times he would stay out all night and drink. Occasionally he would wake us up coming in, but that's the only thing I saw of him. On the weekends he had a bourbon and coke at his side, on the table; he'd be sitting at the corner of the couch, right beside the TV, watching football or basketball or baseball or something. Something was always on the TV to watch, and my brother and I would be outside running around, doing all sorts of stuff.

His crutch now is "I did stuff with you. Remember that T-ball game I played?" There was one day, and there are tons of pictures of it because he had my mother come out and take pictures—I guess 'cause he knew what a jerk he was, and he wanted us to see these pictures, like, "Wow, we really did a lot of stuff with my dad." He always had my mother take pictures when we did anything with him. There was one T-ball game that we did play with my dad one time, and it was very well documented.

That's all I saw of him, so my dad and I didn't really have a relationship. He never came to my swim meets. I was supposed to be in the Olympic trials last year. He never supported that, and that was a huge goal, something I was dedicated to—three practices a day, seven days a week, from the time I was seven years old until the time I was sixteen. He never saw that. If I wasn't swimming, I was at my school being the Student Council president. He never came to those events. When people commented on it, he wouldn't know what they were talking about. He didn't attend my high school graduation. He was in Maryland with his girlfriend.

One of the cruelest acts parents can do, knowingly or not, is to insert their child into the middle of their disputes. Loretta's account of the events leading up to her parents' breakup is ample testimony to the pain children feel when their parents put them in this lose-lose position, and it also shows that this kind of unintentional setup is not something that happens only to younger children.

Loretta, 21 I found out over spring break my sophomore year of college. I went home for spring break, and everything was fine at first—I mean, everything seemed the same. My parents never really fought. In fact, it was odd that they never fought. I went with my dad to the grocery store, and there was a card sitting in the cup holder in his truck, and I was just kind of goofing around, going, "Well, what's this?" And he got real serious, and he said, "Well, there's something I have to tell you, but I shouldn't tell you now." And I can't really remember whether I wanted him to tell me or not, but he finally did tell me. He told me that he was planning to leave Mom and that the card was Mom trying to beg him to stay.

I was hurt. Later, I was angry that he told me like that, because my brothers didn't know. My mom didn't even know that he was definitely leaving. They were still working it through, and I was thrust right into the middle.

So my dad and I, we acted like nothing was wrong. Then three days later I was sitting downstairs with him, and I was kind of crying and kind of upset over it all. And he kept asking me for advice throughout the whole three days, asking, "Well, what should I do? What should I do?" I really feel bad now because I just was kind of supportive. I just didn't know what else to do. I was just like, "Well, if this is what you feel like you need to do, then I guess that's what you need to do," and things like that. I wasn't really saying, "Well, I don't think you should leave," or anything like that.

So my mom found out 'cause I was sitting downstairs with him, and she came downstairs, and she could tell that we were both crying. So she kind of knew that he had told me, and she got really angry and said, "We were gonna tell the kids together if you decided to leave."

So my mom's angry at me because I knew before she did that he was leaving, and she was angry at him because she found out three days later because he didn't want me to say anything.

This was all still my spring break, and my friends were driving on a road trip. They stopped off and stayed at my house for a night. I didn't say anything to them because it was like, "We're not saying anything to anyone," because my mom's mother was visiting. So we spent the whole week acting like everything was fine, and it was no big deal, because my brothers still didn't know at this point.

It was really hard. I think I blanked out a lot of the week. The only thing I remember was my grandparents making us crowd together to take a family picture and how uncomfortable and how sick that made me. You know: "Dad, put your arm around Mom," and I'm just shuddering inside.

Charlotte, 18 I've talked to my mother about divorce, and I've said to her, "Just do it. What are you waiting for?" It's not something that they ever considered. It wasn't an option for them. They just thought other people do that. Bad people do that.

Helaine, 17 They had never been very loving to each other. That was strange because my mom especially has always been very loving, and so it was weird that their relationship wasn't like that. It was always really tense. My dad was always pretty controlling, and so my mom was always pretty nervous about how things were when he was home and making sure that everything was just fine for him. We'd be fine during the day, but then when it was time for Dad to come home, the tension between the two of them kind of affected how my brother and I could do things. It wasn't necessarily that there was anything wrong with my dad coming home or how my dad acted, it was just the tension between the two of them when they were together, especially during the last couple of years.

Joyce, 17 They were pretty much fighters. Mom is more so than Dad, but Dad tends to fight and then leave, and Mom tends to get more and more upset and just go nuts. So Mom would get upset and start going crazy, and Dad would just go for a walk, just leave. A lot of times I went with him. I was like, "Oh, let's go. Let's go for a walk."

Laura, 17 When I was about eleven or twelve, my parents had a lot of marital problems, I think. I mean, they never really told us anything, and I think part of that is really scary. I think it would have been helpful if they had been honest because, like, I knew something was going on. My room was right next to theirs, and I would hear them talking in hushed tones, kind of angry tones, and I honestly thought then they were gonna get a divorce. I was just waiting for them to come and tell me, and then they didn't. I don't know what that was all about or if that arguing was part of what ended it later. It was never really a fight. I never really heard what was going on. Mom would usually leave and go for a walk, crying or whatever, and sometimes one of us would come with her, but she would never say anything or mention anything that had happened or gone on.

Riza, 18 I have a couple of very vague memories. I have a memory of a fight between my parents. All I remember is that I was sitting on a rug in the living room, and one of them was sitting on an armchair, and one was sitting on the couch. And they were talking. They weren't actually yelling, they were talking. And I could sense as a very young child that they were having some sort of argument.

And then I remember my dad's boxes by the door. I remember boxes of records because he had a whole bunch of records. I remember there were two or three different boxes of records, and there were boxes pretty much leading all the way to the door, so it was kind of hard to get in and out of the apartment. And that's all I remember from before the divorce itself. I remember being puzzled by it because I don't think, when I was that young, I really understood what was going on. And I remember asking about the boxes and asking, "Why is Daddy going out?"

Loretta, 21 The signs had been coming more from my dad than my mother. When I went away to college, when I was a freshman, he was always calling me and saying things like, "If anything happens here . . ." He never gave an example or anything. He would just say stuff like "If anything goes wrong at home, you have to stay at school. You can't come home or feel like you need to come home to take care of people. You have to make your own life now." He would say that a lot, and it never really clicked. I mean, at the time I thought, "Oh, he means like if there was an accident or something and someone was in the hospital."

Charlotte, 18 I think they are starting the divorce process partially because I started it. I think that has a lot to do with it. Because I've gotten old enough to be like, "There's something wrong here." But I mean, it's still stressful to have to be the instigator or something like that. It's not a pleasant situation to be in.

Nicole, 19 More than anything they had an extremely power-hungry, controlling relationship, and I guess I know more about my dad doing things that made it seem controlling. He says things all the time about how controlling Mom was, but I guess I didn't see that as much. So I'm not sure if that was just his interpretation or if I'm just hearing the other side more now or what. But I know it wasn't as verbally abusive as some, but it certainly was verbally abusive.

Leroy, 15 I remember times especially when, early on, they would take us to our auntie's house, and they would just go with their friends to, like, Atlantic City, just take little trips for weekends. They just enjoyed being around each other. It was always the two of them. And it was fun.

That's what I think a family is. I think of a daddy in there watching TV, my mom in the kitchen cooking over the stove, my brother washing the cars, my sister helping my mama, and me playing on the steps. That's my idea of family. That's always gonna be my idea of family. That's constructive. If a child doesn't have that, he doesn't have anything. Some people say family is people who are rocking back and forth on the porch, you know, picket fence or whatever. I think of us being in the same house, everybody doing what they do best. So at least I had that once, that type of harmonious feeling. I guess as long as I got that, I'll be all right. They gave me that. They gave me at least ten good years of how a family is supposed to be, so I know.

Like Loretta, children of all ages will often give a parent the benefit of the doubt, attempting to believe all sorts of implausible explanations while ignoring evidence to the contrary, in an attempt to retain their positive image of their parent.

Loretta, 21 I'm from a very small town, and there were rumors about my father having an affair, and Mom had heard these rumors way before me. I believed Dad. I mean, I believed that he wasn't having an affair with this woman. But I think I needed to believe that at the time, and I don't think that was the truth. Because then later I thought about other things, and as early as when I went home for Christmas break, he had really wanted me to meet her. He had insisted that I come to work and meet him to go out to lunch so that I could meet her. At the time I felt a little odd about it, but I really wasn't sure why because he was totally claiming, "Oh, well, she's just a really nice person. We're friends, and I'd like you to meet her." But he'd never wanted me to meet anyone before.

My brothers were obviously hearing the rumors. There's no way really that they could have avoided them. None of us liked her at all, not just because of the rumors. I tried to look past the rumors. Like I said, I was totally believing Dad. "Dad said that this wasn't going on, and I need to be open-minded about this person, because who knows what role this person is gonna play in his life?" or whatever. But I just couldn't keep an open mind, because I felt she was younger than me, she was just really immature, and it made me really uncomfortable to think that he would be with someone like this. It made my brothers uncomfortable because he would act really immature with her. He was acting like someone who wasn't even their dad at all.

I was just trying to view him as someone going through a rough time, and this isn't really Dad. "Maybe someday he'll be okay, but this isn't him." That's how I tried to think about it. But it was hard because up until that time I hadn't gotten to the stage where I stopped idealizing my parents, because we didn't really fight a lot when I was a teenager. We never had any big breaks or big disagreements. We'd always gotten along really well, and I was close to both of them, or at least I thought I was. So it made me realize that he wasn't just my dad, he was also a person.

It was hard to take, because I could look at it that way, but I knew my brothers couldn't. That's what concerned me, especially with my older brother. My younger brother is real forgiving, and he would come around—even when my dad's girlfriend was with him—and act like it was okay, like everything was fine just to be around Dad. But my older brother wouldn't do that. If Dad's girlfriend was there, my older brother wouldn't come. He wouldn't have anything to do with her. He's the one who will always talk for all of us. My younger brother wouldn't come out and say, "I don't like Dad's girlfriend. I don't want to be with her," but my older brother had no problem saying that. And if he knew that Dad's girlfriend was gonna be at an event that Dad had planned for all of us, he'd be like, "That's it, I'm not going."

Charlotte, 18 It is really upsetting to know now that they've contacted attorneys. It's not so much that it surprises me, because it doesn't. But it's still upsetting. You don't want to know that that's true, even though it seems like it is.

They try not to make it apparent, but it's still apparent. It's not like they scream at each other and fight all the time, but it's obvious that they're, like, very reclusive. They were never very close friends, which would have been nice. Maybe they didn't realize that it was obvious to me, but they just don't seem to really like each other. Even though they try not to show it in front of us, but still, it's so obvious. I was never aware of it when I was younger, but I think it's always been that way. I think I just became more aware.

Tom, 12 Things got hectic. I was half asleep. I didn't know what to do because the lights were off, and usually when the lights are off, you go to sleep. I heard them fighting. Mom and Dad were screaming at each other, shrieking at the top of their lungs, arguing over somebody, something. It went on until, I think, ten o'clock, and then my mom went off in a huff. Then I heard my mom come up the stairs. I closed my eyes because I didn't want them to know that I heard. Somebody came in to check, turned on my lights, and then shut them back off and left, and then locked the door of their room.

27

Lance, 13 Everybody was always yelling and screaming. When my sister would talk about them getting a divorce, I'd tell her to shut up. I mean, I didn't want to hear it. It looked like it would be the truth, and I didn't want to hear it. I didn't have any resilience back then.

Charlotte, 18 Even as I started kind of hoping that they would get divorced, I still didn't think they ever would.

Two

THE SEPARATION: Where Are You Going?

> Children are informed about an impending divorce in many
> ways, some appropriate, others less so. A child's reaction,
> while guided to some degree by how he is told, does not
> necessarily conform to expectations. The child's behavior can
> actually mask his true internal reactions. It is the task of the
> parents to try to see if there is something happening
> underneath the mask.
>
> Sometimes the reality of divorce does not hit until the
> separation occurs. Children build their worlds on the
> foundation of Mom and Dad living with them. When a parent
> moves out, it can be crushing for a child. On the other hand,
> sometimes it can be a time of relief, signaling a decrease in the
> disturbing conflict under which the children may have been
> living. It is normal for children to vacillate between both of
> these reactions, and this ambivalence is difficult for children of
> all ages.

Leroy, 15 When your mother and father split up, I don't care what
age you are, if you love them at all, it hurts. It hurts bad.

Gary, 11 I was the first in my grade to get a divorce. My parents
were the first ones to get a separation. Everyone else, you could see
their moms and their dads at the Christmas parties. My mom and
dad, they wouldn't even face each other. If they faced each other and

if it was more than five minutes, they would shriek at the top of their lungs.

Joan, 18 I was probably in fifth grade, still in Catholic school. My mom took me aside and told me that my father and she were going to be separated, that I would still see him, they were just going to be separated. There was much confusion, and there was much crying on her end, hysterics and stuff like that, and there was much crying on my end. I mean, I did a lot of crying in my childhood, throughout junior high, high school—a lot of crying because of this, because I felt so strongly for my parents. The divorce affected me.

Roberta, 16 When Mom left, I was three, in preschool in Colorado. We stayed with Dad for a year. I guess we stayed with him because she thought it would be really selfish for her to leave and take us, because she had nowhere to go, no one to go to, no money, nothing, pretty much a housewife with these two kids and two dogs. She spent the entire year, pretty much my preschool year, getting organized, and that next summer she was in Louisiana, and she sent for us.

Loretta, 21 He was real weird after he first moved out. He didn't have a laundry machine or anything. He would come over when Mom wasn't there and do laundry. Things like that. He would come over and watch TV with my brothers and do laundry, and she got really upset by that because, like, "This is my home now. You left." They got into big fights about that, and he kept doing it. He would go in when no one was there and get a suitcase or something that he wanted. He would do that all the time.

Finally, Mom changed all the locks, and when she gave us all those house keys, she said, "Do not let your dad get this." But that was really weird for me. I came home from college, and my house key didn't work. She didn't even warn me. I was coming home kind of late, and Dad picked me up at the airport, but I couldn't get into my house.

It kind of freaked me out. Just the idea that we had to do that, that we were afraid of my dad, that we were locking my dad out of the house. She put all these locks on, like the chain, this other one that slides over. She had more security than we'd ever had on our house, and it was because of my dad. It was not some stranger out there who was trying to break in. I can see why she was freaked out about him coming in the house all the time when she wasn't there, but the entire thing was really awkward.

Martin, 18 When they separated, sure, I cried. But then I was introduced to a little electronic item called the Game Boy. I think I went through about eight packages of batteries within the first four weeks, I was so absorbed in it. I was using it as a distraction.

Barb, 18 I remember my father walking me to the school bus stop. He had never done that before. It was weird. He would always make us breakfast and everything like that, but he never walked me. He spoke to me with some sort of sparse words of good-bye, saying that things would be the same, that things wouldn't change that much, that I'd still see him, stuff like that.

I climbed onto the bus when it came, and he waved at me when the bus went away, and I waved at him, which was odd because he had never seen me to the bus before, so it was just "Bye, Dad."

When I came back from school, all his things were gone, and he was gone. I didn't know where he was. I didn't know for about a month, because he didn't call the house. I think he was looking for a place to stay. And I cried. I cried so much, and I worried so very much about his safety, about him being lonely. I felt as if I was feeling his loneliness. I guess I was doing a lot of empathic things, stuff that was just not very good for my emotional health.

Finally, he did contact us, and we were able to visit him. I'd been crying so much, so many days. It actually may have been just a week or something, but it felt like a month. When I finally heard from him, it didn't feel any better, it didn't feel any worse. He was still gone, and when we first visited him at his apartment, it was gross. There were big cockroaches, with no shame. You'd turn on a light, and they didn't flinch. They were everywhere, and it was small, dingy. That was what I was fearing, you know? He was living there, and he was eating all this cruddy food from a cafeteria. He brought us there to eat this greasy crap, and when I got home, I cried so much and I worried so much.

Jamal, 20 Several times my dad came to tell me he was moving out. It was never a surprise. You know they're fighting, and you know they'd be doing better apart. The last time he told me he was leaving, I was fourteen. They had been going back and forth for a couple of years, and finally he just said, "I'm moving out."

You know how he told me? He came in my room, and no one ever came in my room, it was so dirty and messy. He said, "I'm moving out," and gave me five dollars. I knew then that he wasn't coming back, because he's real cheap, real tight. I'm cheap just like him. When he gave me that money, I knew, because he never gave me money. I always had to work for the money.

A parent might underestimate the reaction that children, and especially older children, have to the parent who is moving out. This underestimation may help parents cope with their own sense of loss, and it can also help reduce their feelings of guilt for leaving.

Loretta, 21 When I was talking to him in the car and when he was telling me he was leaving, I got the sense from him that he thought it was no big deal. He was bored and unhappy with his life, and all he did was sit in front of the TV when he was home anyway, so he kind of felt like, "Well, your brothers can come and visit me, and they're not gonna notice whether I'm here or not, and I'll be much happier somewhere else." I didn't get the sense from him that he anticipated there would be any real pain. He seemed to think he would hurt my mom, but for everyone else, it would be a relatively easy process, no big deal.

When communication is not clear, children are likely to take on at least some of the responsibility for the breakup, as Wayne did.

Wayne, 17 It wasn't like they told me they were separating. When they did finally tell me, I kind of had it figured out on my own. They weren't getting along too well. I remember it was the summer, and my mom had to be out of the apartment by a certain day. And my dad and I, we hadn't been getting along too well, either, so I knew for sure he wouldn't be moving back in. So I kind of figured it out. I can't say there was a lot of fighting, but we all had our share. Yeah, there was a lot of tension. It just got crazy sometimes.

Nicole, 19 It was a Monday night, and they were arguing, and I heard him packing up his stuff. He came in, sat down, and said, "Well, I'm leaving," and he took off. It was kind of strange. He just took off right then.

For a couple of months, almost until right around the time of the divorce, he would come over every morning after Mom went to work. She'd go to work early, and he'd come over and make us breakfast, so he actually still had time with us. But then when it got closer to the divorce, everything was getting really ugly between the two of them. Mom didn't really want him in the house, because after we left, he was going through our stuff, and things like that.

It got where we'd go out to breakfast once a week. My brother was older and starting high school. He went to school a little earlier than I did, because I was just finishing elementary school. That was always a fun time for Dad and me. There was a restaurant that we went to often. They knew what we would get and what time we would be there, and so when we got there, the food would be coming up for us. It was a lot of fun, good bonding time with Dad.

I'd already felt close to him, I guess, but before that, it was more like we didn't have as much time just set apart that was our time, like our breakfast time. It was more sporadic. Sometimes that's better because we'd be able to go out and play baseball or go fly a kite. We really didn't get as much time after the separation to do the sporadic fun things that we could do before, like sit and read the Sunday comics. But we did have our time that was set apart, so it was kind of a trade-off.

I wouldn't say that we got any closer during the time they were separated because it was just a really hard time. It was a hard time to really know where we stood with things, but it wasn't like all of a sudden he wasn't in my life or anything.

Joan, 18 For the longest time, until the end of my high school years, I was fearing that my father was turning almost into an uncle rather than a father, at least in the way that we related. I didn't know why, what was missing that separated the father from the uncle part. But somehow I thought of him as Uncle Dad or something, although I never verbalized it. That was very worrisome, actually. But what could I do? It's how I felt. I don't feel it as much now that I live with him. I mean, he's my father and stuff. But that was really, really strange, that feeling of Uncle Dad.

Tom, 12 It felt awkward, very awkward before the divorce, because I was never told until the last day. Mom and I flew down to Atlanta to see her family for Thanksgiving. Dad said good-bye to us at the airport. Then we came back up the next Monday, and he wasn't there, he wasn't at home. I asked, "Is he gonna come home tonight?" I always expected him around eight o'clock, when he would usually come home.

Mom said, "He's not gonna come home tonight." And then it was "He's not gonna come home tonight" the next night, and then I asked, "What's really happening?" And she said, "Something's happened. You know how your dad wasn't here a few months ago?" And I just

said, "Yeah." "We got back together then, but this time it's permanent." And I didn't know what "permanent" meant. I said, "What
does that mean?" And she told me.

Helaine, 17 My mom and dad both did counseling to some
degree. They tried to do it jointly, but that was just a bomb. They
would just scream. Therapy was always a time of explosion. They'd just
sit there and yell the whole time, so they ended up switching it over so
that they each had individual therapy. I think it was with the same
counselor, though, so that she could help them together, but not with
them in the same room at the same time. They could not handle it.

And at times they'd go in with several counselors so that they had
her counselor and his counselor, and then they'd just argue in front of
them. I think the therapy did help in general. I think they just needed
to do it separately. I know that with a lot of couples, even though they
don't get along and don't want to live together anymore, that doesn't
mean they can't get along civilly if they have to.

Roberta, 16 After my mom moved out, my dad would put the
barrettes in my hair, and by the time I got to school, they would be out.
So my teacher sent a note home one day saying, "Just send the
barrettes in a bag, and I'll put them in."

And I remember him making fish sticks and hot dogs for dinner a lot.
And Pop-Tarts for breakfast.

*If there is ever a time for parents to weigh their words when talking with their
children, it is during separation and divorce. At a time when a child's world has
become uncertain and untrustworthy, the last thing the child needs is any more
disappointment, as epitomized by Robin's heartbreaking account of her parents'
separation.*

Robin, 18 It was in the summer, and I was nine. I was on a team,
and I went to practice. When I came home, the van was all packed up,

and I was like, "What's going on?" I just came home, and Dad's like, "Hey, I'm leaving," and I was like, "That's not cool." I was very upset. I was pretty much like a daddy's girl, too. I'm not like my mom at all. And he didn't even tell me. My older brothers and sister knew, but I didn't, and my little sister didn't, either, but she was only five. I think I should have been told. It always will be hard for me to remember.

He took me on a walk, but I was just mad. I was like, "No, leave me alone." I mean, he tried as well as he could have, I guess. He said he was going, and he'd be back in two weeks, and I could come with him if I wanted to. But I was upset. He was going just across town, moving into this little apartment. My older brothers and sister went with him. They were leaving with him, too. So they all knew. They were all the ones that I was bonded with. I was totally ditched.

I would have been the first to go because Dad and me, we called each other "spesh" because we were like special friends. We had one of those great relationships, where I didn't really have one with Mom very much at all, and neither did anybody. But Dad didn't want to take my little sister because she was only five. He asked me if I wanted to go with him, but I didn't want him to leave. So I said, "No," thinking that he wouldn't go if I didn't go with him. But then he went anyway. Bad call on my part. So that sucked, but what can you do?

If he had only given me a little while to decide. Plus, I thought he would come back in two weeks, which is what he said. He told me he would be coming back in two weeks. I think he ideally wanted to. I mean, he stuck around for, what, seven years, sleeping on the floor. But if you get an apartment, you're not planning on coming back in two weeks. He got an apartment, not a hotel room, and took all his stuff he needed.

I really didn't think he would leave without me because we were connected. He taught at a community college, and I'd go with him and hand out papers. So I honestly did not think he would go. So when he asked if I wanted to go with him, I said it, "No," and he got tears in his

eyes, and I was just like, "No way. No way are you really gonna go."
Oh, well, what can you do?

I did believe him when he said he'd be back in two weeks. At the end
of two weeks, I sat on the porch for the entire day, and I fell asleep on
the porch. Mom had to yell at me to get me to come inside. So then I
was bitter after that for years and years. I don't think you should do
that. I don't agree with how he did it, but it's all right. I think he was
trying to make it easier for me for that time, but it just made it a lot
worse.

Fred, 9 The reason Mom and Dad divorced is that there are
reactions, you know? Somebody goes "pow!" Blows up. Hits. When I
was little, when I was two, two and a half, I bit my dad on the finger,
and he had a reaction. He threw a blow at me, and my mom got mad at
him and asked him for a divorce. When I was growing up, when I was
three, four, five, I didn't like to be with my dad a lot. Right now I like
him a lot because he is my friend. I like him just as my dad, not my
friend. See, I was a mama's boy. When you are really little, like five or
four or three, you're like a mama's boy, and you don't like to be with
your father that much, and sometimes it's because you remember some
harmful blows that he gave you.

Three

DIVORCE: The Big Event

The legal milestone of the divorce may have little meaning for a child, or it may have plenty. If the parents live together right up until the divorce becomes final, then the divorce and the separation are the same event for the children. However, a divorce will often come months, or even years after the initial separation. How this final legal step affects a child usually depends on how the parents have managed the various divorce events up until that time. How the parents themselves are affected by this step, psychologically and emotionally, also influences how the children react to it.

Barb, 18 The divorce was nothing. I mean, the divorce was after a separation of, like, how many years? Suddenly they said, "We're divorced," and I'm like, "Okay." It was just a formality. What was really odd to me was that a couple of months after the official date of the divorce, even though they had been separated a long time, my dad got remarried. That was weird.

Jamal, 20 I never knew when they were actually divorced. They tried to keep me out of it, but they couldn't. What they tried to do was work it out together. They tried to settle their own differences like grown people, but they just really did outgrow each other. The idea of a family kept drawing them back together. My mom had two kids from a previous marriage, he had two kids from a previous marriage, but I was the only kid between them. Only my mom's kids lived with us, so what we did have was a family. There was no problem, besides, between them two, between my mother and my father, so fifty percent of the time they were happy, and the other fifty percent of the time they were mad at each other. They just tried to keep it together. Like, "That's what a family is supposed to be, and I'm not gonna give up."

Around the time of the divorce, it started being more like seventy-five/twenty-five not getting along. It just built up. As a matter of fact, I remember times when it got so bad that it was ninety/ten. But they were just so content, they stayed together. I guess they had their problems arguing and whatnot. It just got to be too much on my mom, I guess. It didn't too much bother my father. He's like me. I guess that's where I got it from. I don't show emotions. It just doesn't ever come out, especially when I'm hurting. I can brush it off real easy, I guess from seeing him do it. Don't let nothing bother you, just keep on working. Not work through emotions but just work. Go to work—you know what I'm saying? Just let it fall off.

Work was where a lot of their problems came from. My mom had started working when I was in first grade. It was three kids, two adults, and his business was just getting started, so money was tight. When you got kids and your finances aren't right, you just put a lot of tension on the marriage. You have debt, you worry a little more. When you're sharing that responsibility with somebody, I guess you're gonna try to take some of your anger, your anxiety, out on them.

Tom, 12 The reason they divorced supposedly was because of another woman, which I didn't really like.

Robin, 19 There were three court dates when they were supposed to finish the divorce, and every time Mom would go, and then she'd come home and she'd be like, "Well, it didn't happen." They just kept having to go back, and it took over a year. I was almost eleven when they actually got divorced. Dad wanted to do it on my birthday, and I got really mad at him. Of course, my mom came home and said, "He wants to do it on your birthday," and it ended up like it was actually gonna be my birthday. It was like a bad birthday present. But Mom didn't help things at all, looking back on it now. But what can you do?

Al, 16 My parents get along a lot better now than before Dad moved out and they got divorced. He'll come over for dinner and stuff.

Nicole, 19 They signed the divorce papers two weeks before my eleventh birthday, on their twentieth wedding anniversary. It's pretty ironic. I guess the timing came as a surprise. I don't think we had really thought about it.

Wayne, 17 They never separated before the divorce. The divorce was when it happened. It just didn't make any sense to me. I didn't understand why, because it was real complicated. It's hard to explain what it was like. See, basically the problem was they'd always fight. My dad would go to the bar a lot and stuff. They'd just get into a lot of fights over stuff like that. He'd say he'd be coming home at one time, and he wouldn't come home till later. Stuff like that. My mom decided she wanted to move, so she moved in with my grandmother.

One of the suggestions often given to parents when they are divorcing is that they be appropriate models for grieving. For example, many parents avoid crying in front of their children during this time, fearing that they will upset them even further. The message the child is receiving, however, is that crying or feeling bad about the whole experience is not acceptable. When parents allow themselves to cry in front of the child, the child is being given permission to cry. This comment from Helaine shows that it also helps when parents talk about what it is they are crying about, so the child will not misunderstand or misinterpret his parents' tears.

Helaine, 17 Right after the divorce, I guess Mom was having a hard time with the divorce and going through a period where she'd cry over anything. She was always so sad about stuff and was going through such a hard time, but it was difficult for me, and I always felt like, "Well, gosh, what's the matter? Doesn't she realize she still has us?"

For Loretta and her brothers, their mom's tears served as the center for their grieving together.

Loretta, 21 Mom spent a lot of time crying in the closet. There's a dark corner in the back of the closet, and she spent a lot of time in that closet, crying. She would go in there because she wouldn't want us to know that she was home, and we would go around the house looking for her. Inevitably we would find her there, and we would all sit in the closet with her. She never became fundamentally irresponsible or anything like that. She was just upset, and sometimes she couldn't take care of my brothers, maybe because she was upset, but I think they could see that because they always emerged to be there for Mom when she needed them. They were always in the closet with her, or if she wanted them to go somewhere with her because she was upset, they would go, and if she wanted one of them to drive, he would. Things like that. Which is part of what made it hard for Dad, too. I think he felt like she had the boys under her thumb. And he was driving them away because he was being irresponsible. But I think he sort of felt like she was taking them from him.

Elliot, 11 It was actually nobody's fault. It's just that my mom didn't like where she was living. They still loved each other, but they just had to live the life they wanted to have.

Kids are naturally curious. If there is information you do not wish them to see, do not underestimate their abilities to ferret it out.

Martin, 18 I got in trouble for reading the settlement. It was in the word processor. I was like, "Oooh, okay, what's this?" I was in my little prepubescent hacker stage, so I opened up the file and started reading through it. And it was just like, "Parents will give this and that," and I was just like, "Oh, okay, this is a legal thing. Whatever." And then my mom walked in, and she said, "What are you reading?" I'm like, "Uh, nothing." And she kind of yelled at me a little. And I was like, "It's no big deal. I don't care."

This struck me as an interesting image from a child who wants his parents to stay together. His poem's solution seems to be that instead of drowning in the divorce, his parents will save themselves by sharing love. Then again, you might have a different interpretation.

Eric, 6 Want to hear a poem? Here it is. Once upon a time, there was a river, and they jumped in it when they got divorced, and it was called a divorce love river. And then they all went into it, and jumped into it, and they can't swim, so, gulp, they drank the river.

Wayne, 17 They said it was an amicable divorce or something like that. He still comes in the house. I still see him a lot. I mean, I don't see why they got divorced. I was upset about it, but in a way I wasn't because when they would fight, it would be like they would just keep arguing, like they didn't know when to stop.

Nick, 17 It's been so long, like thirteen years, since they've been divorced. It just seems like they were never married.

Winny, 12 Sure, I definitely wonder why my parents got a divorce, definitely. My mom and dad never talk about it with me. They probably would if I asked. I don't know why I don't ask.

Riza, 18 I remember a conversation about the divorce with my dad. My mom didn't go into long, emotional conversations. She really kept with the problem-solution–type of thing. She wouldn't go into all the reasoning and this and that, which was kind of nice if my mom and I ever had a fight. It was sort of like, "I'm mad at you." "I'm mad at you, too." I'd go to my room and sit around a little bit. I'd get over it, and then we'd get along. And I really liked that.

With my dad, it would go on for hours. "Why am I mad at you? And what are the reasons for this?" And all this psychological stuff. I'd be like, "Hey, I'm kind of mad at you, and you're kind of mad at me, and I didn't do the dishes. Sorry." But on the other hand, I could have these long conversations with my dad. So we did talk about it sometimes, because he'd ask me how I felt about it. With all these things, with his various marriages and divorces and all this stuff, he'd always share with me and see how I felt about it. Got my input. We've always been close that way. Always asking.

Roberta, 16 Mom at one point thought about getting their marriage annulled, and I was asking Dad how he felt about that. And he said, "No. If she really wants it done, I can understand because she wants to go back to the Catholic Church and be accepted officially. But I'm not going to say to you that our marriage didn't happen, because that's what an annulment is, to say it officially didn't happen. Your mother and I were married ten years before we got divorced, and for me they were ten good years. I have you and your brother, and saying the marriage never happened is saying that you guys never happened." And I thought that was really cool. And I agree with him on that.

Fred, 9 When my parents got a divorce, I felt like a no-one. Everybody at the "Y" when I was little, all their parents were getting a divorce. Some kids teased me about it. What was good when my parents got a divorce is that they stopped arguing. I didn't have to hear "Shut up, you," and stuff. I have friends whose parents are divorced, but I never talk to them about it because I feel so crappy and cruddy about it. You feel like shit when your parents divorce, but after a while you feel better. But I still don't really feel comfortable because my parents got a divorce.

Christina, 19 In grade school, I remember being really upset, being really defensive and angry about my parents getting a divorce.

Loretta, 21 Mom felt like when they got divorced, that was one thing, but she was trying to be friends with him for the kids, and she wanted him to still be a parent to us. She wanted him to be involved in decisions with us. She would call him and say, "Our son did this. I wanna talk to you about it. Can we?" But it just wasn't working, and he just wasn't a parent at all. He was totally off the deep end and always off with his girlfriend. He never called my brothers. My younger brother saw him because he would go over there, but I don't think my older brother saw him or spoke to him for several months, living in the same town, just because Dad was too involved with his girlfriend to call.

Wayne, 17 It still doesn't make any sense to me. I don't see why they got divorced. I mean, they get along so well now. I guess they couldn't live together. That was like the main thing, so I guess I'm not pissed at them as long as they're happy.

Four

SELF-BLAME: Is It My Fault?

Not all children blame themselves for their parents' divorce, but many do. It is certainly recommended that you tell them repeatedly it is not their fault, but that does not mean they will stop worrying about it. One good idea is to avoid arguing or even quietly disagreeing about anything having to do with the child while she is within earshot. Hearing her parents in dispute over her is one of the surest ways to get a child's mind to generalize that all the trouble is because of her. Presenting a united front, with disagreements worked out away from the child, is the best approach. Getting the child into a support group, as discussed in the Introduction, can also help.

Darnell, 14 I heard that a lot of kids blame themselves but, naw, I don't. Sometimes they'd get into fights where it would be my fault. Like my mom would get on me, and my father didn't know what was going on. He would come home and see me crying, and he'd say, "What did you do now?" I knew what they were arguing about because they were so loud. Where's this money going? Where's that money going? They got into it maybe twice over me, but I knew what I did was wrong. I messed up. My mama got on me, my father got on my mom, and my mother got on my father.

Ted, 12 It was sad when they got divorced. It was really tough. I was ten. I'm used to it now. I read in a book that it wasn't my fault. That helped, because I was wondering.

Loretta, 21 They both claimed the reason their marriage really fell apart was that they focused on us so much, and they spent so much time being parents and being there for us and whatever that they didn't spend enough time on their relationship with each other.

Carie, 15 Did I blame myself for their divorce? Never. And everyone's always so shocked when I say that, but I didn't at all. I always blamed it on my older brother. I swear to God. You can ask my friend. She asked, "Do you feel guilty?" I said, "No, it's my brother's fault." I think that's one of the reasons I liked having an older brother, because there was always someone to blame. But I never thought, I still don't think, it was my fault at all.

Roy's is an interesting situation. In all of my interviews with children, both for this book as well as for the court, it was the first instance where I heard of a parent's actually telling a child of any age that the divorce was the child's fault, that it was because of the child's behavior. I listened with a mixture of horror and incredulity. Could this mother have really said this to her son? Not surprisingly, he was very distressed about it, though he did his best to hide his pain, especially considering that my interview with him was a dual interview with a friend of his. I encouraged Roy to discuss this perception of his with his mother or, at the very least, if he felt uncomfortable doing so, with his father, since his parents seemed to get along well.

Several days later I received a phone call from Roy's mother. She sounded close to tears. I was relieved to hear that Roy had broached this subject with his mother, who was horrified to find out that her son had been harboring the impression that he had caused their marital problems. She described a conversation she had had with Roy where Roy had misunderstood a point she was making. He had arrived at his misinterpretation without his mother's having any idea. She was very thankful that Roy had brought it up again, allowing her to set the record straight, and she called to

let me know that Roy now understood that the marital problems and divorce had
nothing to do with him.

This incident underlines just how important it is that parents be very clear and
careful when discussing divorce-related issues with their children. Even so, children
may reach their own, often erroneous, conclusions, making it doubly important that
the lines of communication between parent and child remain open.

This excerpt from the interview with Roy took place before he had shared his
concerns with his mother.

Roy, 17 I was a pretty selfish kid. I was an only child, and my mom
would usually give me whatever I wanted. When I was little, I guess I
could have been a part of the reason that they were always fighting,
because I'd come home from school, and my mom would be like, "Do
your homework," and I'd be like, "I'll do it later." Me and my mom
would argue a lot. So then my dad would kind of get into the argument.
My mom said to me once—I couldn't believe she said it to me—that I
was the reason they got divorced. That's why I'm confused, because I
might have been tough when I was little and stuff, but to say something
like that to your son? I mean, how was that supposed to make me feel?
It was my fault? As I said, I used to be selfish, but not to the point
where something like that would happen. I didn't think I could be, at
that age, that much of an asshole.

I used to be bad, but most of the fights between them would be
because he'd be out late and stuff, and she wouldn't know where he
was or something like that. I was like, "Why did you guys really get
divorced? It doesn't make any sense. You guys still always see each
other. Everything's fine." She's like, "Well, you're the reason." I'm
like, "What?" It doesn't make sense. I try not to think about it
too much because I don't want that to bother me. Even if it was,
I wouldn't say it to my son. How the hell does she think I feel that
she said that to me? Thanks a lot. So, obviously, I ruined your
marriage?

Tom, 12 When I was little, I thought the divorce was my fault, but it's sort of out of my mind. I don't remember. It's probably just the guilt of it.

Nick, 17 It wasn't my fault. That's all their problem. I've heard so many different stories from my mom, but she's the kind of person who makes things out to be way worse than they are. So I don't really believe anything she says right now. I'm waiting to hear from my dad, because he's always been, like, not blowing things out of proportion. I think the kids with the hardest problems are the kids who think it's their fault. I don't ever remember thinking that way. Both my mom and my dad sat down with me at different times and told me it wasn't my fault. I think if the parents really sat down and explained to their kids—as long as they say it's not your fault, you won't worry about it.

Fred, 9 I think they would have gotten a divorce even if I hadn't bitten his finger that one time. But I still feel sometimes that the divorce is my fault.

Five

PUTTING THE CHILD IN THE MIDDLE: Caught in the Web

One of the cardinal sins of divorce is to put the children in the middle of the dispute. This can be done in a thousand ways, from making the child a messenger, to ridiculing the other parent in the child's presence, to making a child take sides. It is not only parents who do this. Friends and family members loyal to one side can lose sight of the child's dilemma and expect the child's loyalties to jibe with their own. An off-the-cuff wisecrack from a child's uncle about the uncle's ex-sister-in-law, if overheard by the child, can cut into a kid's heart like a razor.

Nicole, 19 I hated being in the middle. They still say things to me now, seven years after the divorce, about the other parent, and they expect me to laugh at a bad joke about them or to say something bad about them or to agree with something bad that's said about them. That's just a horrible thing to make somebody do, because they both know that I still care a lot about both of them. So that's always a strange thing to have to deal with. You know they're expecting you to react in a certain way, but you don't really know how to react. It's like, "Well, sure, that might be a funny joke in general, but that's really cutting against my mom."

I have often warned parents who are embroiled in a custody or visitation war to avoid turning their kids into little wishbones. This account of what happened to Jamal is the closest I have come to seeing this actually happen.

Jamal, 20 We were on the porch, and they had gotten into it. My mom grabbed me, and then my father grabbed my other arm, and she was pulling this way, and he was pulling that way. That's when I knew these people weren't staying together. They were really tugging on me. They were like, "Come on!" to me, and I couldn't. I was six. I didn't know what was going on, 'cause they'd always gone downstairs to fight. So here I was facing the neighbor's house, and they were just tugging back and forth. My dad wasn't giving up. I didn't know what to do. I don't know if he let go or if my mom slipped on the porch, or she tugged harder. And he was angry. I guess I was scared a lot.

Roberta, 16 One time, it was around Christmas time, and he was leaving. We were going to say good-bye to him, and Mom hugged him. And I was like, "Hmmm." Later I said, "Wow, you hugged him. What's up with that?" And she said, "Well, life's too short for your dad and me to make your life miserable. We might as well get along because we were married, we did have kids. Why should we sit here and fight in front of the two of you?"

They've always been pretty cool like that. They buy each other Christmas presents still. Of course, when he's over here, it's kind of uncomfortable for him, for obvious reasons. There's a different husband, a new territory, tension. So he doesn't usually stay around. But he'll come over for dinner, or we'll all go out to dinner or something like that. So they tolerate each other.

Riza, 18 They wouldn't talk about problems when I was around. They might call each other during the day when I was at school. I never heard any of it. Thinking back on it, maybe every once in a while I'd hear something, especially in later years when I could understand it.

But there'd be little, tiny, teeny, subtle things. Like my mom would say something about my dad that I could completely relate to, so I'd say it back. Like, "Oh, you know when he goes off on those really long speeches." That kind of thing. And I could completely relate to it. So I'd kind of joke around. Or my dad would say something about the way my mom handles things, and I'd sort of nod and kind of relate because I knew that that's the way she was. As I got a little older, I learned to identify exactly what they were doing.

Divorce court is no place for a child. Going to court can be a rotten experience for adults and can be downright injurious to a child if it is not handled with sensitivity. Even when a child's appearance in court is treated with care, it can still be a terrifying event. Taking a child to court should happen only if it is absolutely necessary. Robin's case presents a good example of when a parent should not pull a child into court.

Robin, 19 They'd always go to the little court place. A couple of times I got dragged along. I have no idea why. I've been looking back on stuff more and thinking how I was influenced by Mom and didn't even realize it. And Dad, too, sometimes, but more so Mom just because I lived with her. I was thinking the other day, and I was like, "You know, I didn't have to go." My little sister never went, but Mom was always like, "Come on, let's go." Then I'd have to sit and watch, and that always made Dad mad. Dad would say, "Robin, why are you here?"

I was being dragged down there to watch them fight over stuff. I think Mom did it on purpose. I never had to talk to anybody. I just had to sit there and watch. Makes you wonder now. Like, "Hmm, why did I have to go?" I think that was Mom's way of trying to make him look bad, like "Look at your dad. He's so mean." But I didn't have that opinion. She knew that I was daddy's little girl more than any of my older brothers or sisters.

So that was really, really mean. Everyone would get mad when I would show up—court personnel and this lawyer, I think it was my dad's lawyer. He took me once into a room, and he was just like, "Why are you here?" And, of course, me being all defensive, I was like, "Oh, I wanted to come." One time I didn't even know where we were going. I was just like, "Aw, man. I hate going here." So that time I said, "I don't even know why I'm here," and the lawyer was just like, "Oh." But then I said, "No, I wanted to come," because then I was afraid they'd yell more. It was all so stupid. Parents get very immature.

Though Helaine wished she had known more about the divorce, her parents were probably right in sharing only some of the information.

Helaine, 17 I'm the type who really likes to know what's going on. I want to be told straight. Still, people will say things, or my mom will say something, and then she'll give me only half the story. Or my dad will say something, but I'll hear only part of it. So to this day I wonder if something really happened a certain way or if there is more to a story. One of them will say it was a physically abusive relationship. "Gosh, it was?" I know it was a verbally abusive one, and so I will just be like, "I was right there in the house. Why didn't I know this?"

They'll just mention things that I remember, little parts. I'll remember an especially bad fight, and they'll say something that happened after they sent us out of the room. And I'll be like, "Well, gosh, how come I couldn't hear that? How come I didn't know enough to come down and protect her?" I still feel like I don't quite know the full story. I don't know if I ever will.

Barb, 18 I was very much their conduit, their mouthpiece, and I still am in some ways. It tore me apart, my senior year of high school especially, with the college stress and everything. I had to start talking about, like, "When did you buy the home? When did you first come to the United States? How much did you buy the home for?" Things that I had to discuss for financial aid purposes. These were things they both had to discuss together, things that I had to get from them together that they had to remember collectively, that they couldn't remember by themselves.

I was going absolutely nuts because it was just childish. They couldn't or wouldn't speak to each other. My first year at college, I was completely flipping out, crying all the time, and it was awful. Finally, I just told them, "No more." But it still remains. I was always their buffer.

No matter what the age, a child in the middle cannot win, as Loretta's experience exemplifies.

Loretta, 21 I always felt like I had to defend Dad because Mom was always so angry, and she was always attacking him and accusing him of this and that. And my brothers were always "Dad did this and Dad did that," so I felt like I had to defend him because I was trying to even things out and trying to keep things so that there was some hope that later on they could work on their issues with Dad, and things would be okay. So I was constantly trying to present his side, but it got to the point where they thought that I was on his side and that I just didn't understand. And I'm sure I didn't because I wasn't there, I was at school.

So that went on all during the summer I was in Japan. I talked to them on and off. It's weird—the times I've been a mess and the times I've been okay. Like during spring quarter, I was pretty much a disaster, and I ended up taking only three classes, and I just kind of threw myself into my classes and tried to ignore what was going on at home. But I was upset all the time. Whenever I wasn't thinking about my classes, I was upset. And then that summer I was better. The only time I was upset that summer was right after I called them. I was so far away and in a completely different country, so it wasn't so immediate.

Nicole, 19 One time we had a neighbor call up and say, "Oh, so he comes over while you're at church on Sundays, huh?"

"No, he doesn't."

"Yeah, he comes in every Sunday and drives his car into the garage and shuts the garage door, goes in for an hour or so, and then comes back out."

"Oh really?"

And so my mom ended up looking for stuff, and some of her papers were missing. And the camera that he had wanted and hadn't gotten was gone. Things like that. Lots of stuff.

So that was strange, because it's hard for me to know what to do about things like that. I hear my mom saying things, and I wanna say, "Hey, look, that's my dad. I still get along with him. I still care a lot about him. I don't wanna know these things about him." I'm not sure who to believe about things like this, because of course he wouldn't admit to those things. So how do I know where to draw the line? Then, on the other hand, my dad always says things like, "Oh, your mother did this and she did that. She turned all these people against me," and things like that. I have a hard time dealing with that side, too, because I'm extremely close with my mom, so I don't wanna hear bad things about her.

Even now we get pulled to some degree, but at least I'm old enough that I can just say, "Hey, look, let's just drop it. I don't wanna talk about this. You know that I care about her" or "I care about him. I don't wanna know. Keep that between the two of you and get on with it." It seems like my mom has gotten on with it a lot better than my dad has. He's still pretty bitter about all of it, and I think he's had a hard time really getting past it.

My mom stayed in our church, and my dad left. My mom was always more involved in our church than my dad was, so all the church friends sided with my mom and not my dad. He became a bad guy in a lot of people's eyes. And if you consider that we go to a church with two hundred and fifty people, that's plenty of people to all of a sudden have completely dislike you and not talk to you. They see you in the store and they turn and walk the other way, pretending they don't see you.

That makes it difficult on us kids, because then we see these people, and we've heard my dad say, "I ran into so and so in the store the other day, and they wouldn't even talk to me. They turned and walked out." And then when you see them that next weekend, you're like, "Oh, great. They were really rude to my father who I care a lot about." It ends up really hurting the kids and ends up hurting the relationship with everybody involved. Whereas I think that someone can be supportive of one of the two parents and be good friends with that parent, and really help them get through it, but I think that that person doesn't have to carry the hatred or the bitterness toward the other parent that the first parent has. That makes it all the more muddled up.

Roberta, 16 I'm "Switzerland." I had to write a religion paper the other day about certain steps that you take to avoid war. I was supposed to apply it to a situation, and I applied it to living with my parents. And my last sentence said, "I'm completely and totally a Switzerland when it comes to them." It's like, "You say your thing and you say your thing, and I'm not going to get involved." It's not that there's no compromising, it's just that they split up and both have their opinions. They're both pretty cool about not bashing each other to me.

If and when to divorce is a decision that parents make. Children should not be put in positions where they must make decisions about how to interact with one or the other parent. The children have no choice in the matter of their parents' divorce, and they should not have to make any decisions on how divorce events progress. Even if Loretta's parents were no longer partners in marriage, they were unwitting and equal partners in forcing their daughter into the middle of their divorce.

Loretta, 21 My mom always claimed that she didn't want to get divorced and that she kept asking Dad to go for counseling to try to work things out, and my dad was just kind of like, "No, I don't want to. I'm just leaving." My mom accused me of okaying his leaving. That was a hard thing to deal with. It really hurt. She said, "You know, he left because you're his favorite, and you're in college now, so he had no reason to stay around here. And if you hadn't been supportive of his leaving, he wouldn't have left."

I admit my initial reaction to him was one of support, but I didn't mean to put myself on his side. I was trying to be neutral. I was just trying to be "Well, if this is what you've decided to do, then I'm not gonna scream and yell at you and tell you not to." I mean, what good would it do? But I think it was interpreted by him and by her as support, because he wanted to see it that way. I mean, clearly it would be helpful to him if he had support, and so I think it was easy to misinterpret my trying to be neutral.

There are a lot of things that I would do differently. I regret a lot of decisions that I made.

Barb, 18 When I was in high school, my mother had a notion in her head that she wanted to rekindle the fires or something, even though my father was somewhere in a divorce with his second wife. She wanted to get back together for financial reasons. I mean, it just makes more sense financially, because after divorce there are two different households, and it's really expensive.

So she told me, which floored me so much, "Barb, go tell your father to come back home, that we want him back in the family again and that we'll go out together, we'll take vacations together with the money that we have, and we'll start again." I told my mother that I didn't think that this was something I was supposed to be saying, that I didn't know how to say that. She wanted me to tell him that she still loved him very, very much, and stuff like that.

I cried and I cried. I talked to my best friend. She has listened to this all the time. I've always called her up and cried about it, and she's been kind of my therapist.

And I had to do it. I mean, I had to go and say, "Dad, can you come back to the house? Can you come back to live in the family?" And he was like, "That's ridiculous. It's over," and all this stuff. And it hurt. It was very painful. It was very messed up. And I know it's pretty sad that it took me this long to do so, but in the last year and a half or so I've been trying to set my limits on what I will and will not relay to the other parent. I'm actually starting to scold them: "You're being completely childish. My God, just pick up the damn phone and talk to each other. I mean, you only have to talk to each other regarding this one issue. It's just for the sake of my brother and me. That's all you have to speak to." It just doesn't work that way. It's not that easy. They're too set in their ways.

And most times it's financial. That's the only thing they have to speak about. Why must it be this difficult? The reasons they gave me before about my being their speaker, their conduit, they said it was because it was always that Dad always listens to me. Mom would say, "When Dad and I talk to each other, we just start fighting, and then we can't speak to each other." Then Dad would tell me, "I don't want to talk to your mom. We don't get anything solved. You talk to your mom, you know her better, you've lived with her," or something like that. It's always these little excuses.

Recently, I just got very, very angry at both of them. But when I ask them to speak to each other regarding an issue, either it will not be addressed or the importance of the issue will start escalating as time goes on. At which point I start complaining, and there will be some very curt conversations. But they can't do it. They just can't.

Robin, 19 Mom clings to religion. She gave me this religious thing one time. "Put this under your dad's bed." So I said okay. And I got caught doing it, so I got into huge trouble because I was in my dad's room, under his bed. I was like, "Oh, no." And he said, "What are you doing?" What do you say? That's Mom's fault. Pretty hypocritical, I think.

Riza's parents had as amicable a separation and divorce as any child could hope for. In this excerpt she is put in a position of making some very big decisions. She was at an age where her input might have been appropriate, considering her maturity and the fact that her parents would have been supportive of her decisions. Still, putting her completely in charge of these decisions might have been too much, a conclusion her parents eventually reached. Even in this best-case scenario, it was still a stressful experience for Riza.

Riza, 18 My mom and stepdad came to me and said, "We're moving in a month. Where do you want to go?" There were all these options, because they were leaving the country. I could leave in a month with them—at that point I was in seventh grade—and I could leave at the end of the school year. I could leave at the end of junior high school, eighth grade. I could stay permanently with my mom. I could leave with them and come back for high school. I had all these options. I talked to my mom, then I talked to my dad. All my life he had really wanted me to live with him, so while he didn't really mean to pressure me, it was like, "Well, I'd really like it if you came and lived with me, but it's completely your choice." Great.

So I felt kind of stuck in the middle a little bit, pretty much the only time that ever happened. My parents were really good about that. They're one of the cases of a good divorce. They don't have to like each other, but they both like me, so it works out. It was really nice, because if there was ever anything going on between them, it went completely over my head, so I had nothing to do with it. That was the only time where I felt a little tension.

But after thinking about it for a while, we kind of came to the decision at the same time. I was going to say my choice, and just then they said that maybe it was a little too much pressure to put on me. It was sort of like choosing between your mom and your dad. Well, it wasn't really, because I had all these options. But it was very close to asking me to do that. I didn't even want it to get that close.

We all decided that it was making me make a decision that I

shouldn't be making. So they decided, and it was the decision that I was about to make if I had to make it myself. It really worked out well. We all kind of think alike.

Loretta, 21 For a while Dad was sitting near Mom at my brother's basketball games, and she would really freak out about that, which I can understand. So that was awkward, like, "Where do they sit?" So now they sit in completely different stands. "I'll go sit by Dad for a while, then I'll go sit by Mom for a while," and it's a whole tug of war thing again. And I feel bad for my brothers because they put up with it all the time.

Christina, 19 My sister wrote Dad this letter, and she actually said in the letter that I hated him. I had no reason to have any other feelings toward him, and I don't think that Mom tried to turn us against him, but obviously she had no reason to speak well of him.

After my sister wrote that letter, he did regain contact with me. We went and visited him. It really struck me at the time that he had no clue how to relate to me. I just remember being on a Flying Boppo ride, and Dad started doing these stupid things people do with little kids, like, "Ha, ha, isn't this funny?" I was eleven or twelve already, and I was like, "Whatever."

Sophie, 18 I don't know whether my mom has gotten on with it as much as my dad has. She'll say things once in a while. I've actually said to her, "Get over it. It's been seven years. Quit being so bitter. Just drop my dad, forget about him, and just get on with it." It seems like her reaction to a lot of things is "Oh, well, that's your father's influence on you," and I feel like I'm my own person. "Get over the fact that my father is the one I live with. Get over the problems you have with him."

She tells me she can't. She tells me that it's impossible, that it's a futile wish, that it hurt her too much to be able to get on with it. A couple of years ago she wouldn't have accepted my saying things like that. That was usually the fuel for any argument my mom and I would have—her problem with my dad or her saying something about my dad—and I would just say, "I don't wanna hear bad things about somebody that I care so much about, from either side. I don't wanna have to deal with that." And I don't feel that we should have to.

Barb, 18 My mother would say, "Go tell your dad that you need money for clothes, you need to go to school. And tell him that your brother needs some more medication."

I would go to my father and say this, and I would have the terrible emotional stress of having to say this as a child. I am still very uncomfortable asking Dad for money. I don't even know how to do it anymore. He takes it almost as an accusation or something. I would receive his emotional response as if I was my mother, and I would react and try to argue my mother's side. Then my father would say this and that, and then finally maybe he would make an ultimatum of sorts. I would go back and relay this to my mother, and my mother would react toward me angrily as if I were my father.

As a child I felt so much for my parents, almost as if I was my parents. I imagined I was my father, and I cried at the loneliness. I cried sometimes as if I were my mother. I did this for a very, very long time. I always had to deal with this back-and-forth stuff for everything, but my brother never had to do any of this.

Robin, 19 Mom always says random stuff like "He has so much hate in him. Just look at him." And when there was that kind of opportunity to look at him, of course he would be making a mean face. So was Mom. And he was always mad at me, and I was always mad at him. So of course I believed it. I was like, "Yeah, he is."

At some point one or both of Loretta's parents should have told her that she should stay out of the conflict and allow them to hash it out. Unfortunately for Loretta, that message has yet to be delivered.

Loretta, 21 Mom would call me: "Your father did this and that." I'd talk to my brothers: "Dad did this to me, he did that to me." Then I'd talk to Dad, and Dad would be like, "Well, that's not exactly what I did. I actually did this and that." I was far away at school, but I was still in the middle, 'cause I'm like, "Well, did you tell them this?" "No." So that just put me more in the middle, and then I would call my brothers and say, "Well, Dad did tell me that he didn't mean it in that way," but they got to where they didn't believe me, understandably, because Dad wasn't telling it to them. He was telling it through me, and it got to the point where they were real angry at me for being on Dad's side when I felt like I wasn't on anyone's side. It just got real confrontational.

Cassandra, 19 It's a shame, because I'd really like to have some sort of a relationship with my father, but he's just absolutely impossible. This last fight, he was trying to tell me that he and my mom were never really married and all this stuff. He was accusing her of all this stuff that never happened, and he's just a big liar. And I said, "Well, if this is the way it's going to be, then forget it," and hung up.

Nicole, 19 They often try subconsciously to make us take sides. I don't think they say, "Oh, here, let me try to pull her my way."

Barb, 18 Before, I would work so hard to get an issue resolved. I would go back and forth between them repeatedly. If I cared anything about my brother's welfare, whether it was educational or finances or something, or if I cared anything about my own stuff, it just needed to be done. Otherwise, how else would it be done? So I did my best to do that, but now, at this point, I tell you, I don't feel guilty. Well, I do in a way, but then it's more anger than guilt. There's always the feeling that it's your family. How can you just say no? You have to do things to help the family. You can't just abandon your family. Responsibility within the family and my role in there is just very confusing.

Loren, 15 "If you can't win with me, that's your only option." That's one thing a lot of people who have two parents don't have to deal with. It's different with divorced parents, because parents play the kids in different ways, but they do it in marriages, too. That's something that I never had. Sometimes I wish there was a second opinion. "No, you can't do that." "But Dad said I could." I didn't have that. I didn't have any form of appeal.

Fred, 9 They don't get along too good, but they still get along as friends. Sometimes my mom calls my dad a kook. I learn real slowly, and I call that a learning disability, and my dad has a learning disability. She says, "You don't have a learning disability. Your father does! He's a kook!" She was saying something about him and she was just joking, but at the same time, because of the way she said it, I don't think she was. I said loudly and clearly, "My father is not a kook." I don't like it when people make fun of him.

Nicole, 19 When they were dividing up property, they had to make lists of all the property assets and then mark down who they thought should get each item, so the lawyers could sit down and go back and forth. My dad put on there that he would give my mom the gardening shed if he could have something else, and we hadn't had a gardening shed for eight years. He had no idea. He put the pool on there that we hadn't had for six years. He was extremely disconnected from the family, or else he was just trying to make it look as if he was being generous so he could get other things.

Things had always been kind of strange with stuff like that. A couple of months before the divorce we really wanted a microwave, and my dad didn't want to spend the money. So my mom and my brother and I spent months getting ready for a yard sale and ended up selling enough of our own things, like our own clothes and toys and things, so that we could get the microwave. Then during the divorce my dad tried to get that, and it was just strange that he was trying to take things away that my brother and I had worked for.

It was tense. My dad decided one day that he wanted the big color TV, and so he and some of his friends walked in the door when my brother and I were watching cartoons. They just came in and took the TV right out from where we were watching it. We were close with our dad—it's not like we had a strained relationship with him—and we were like, "Why are you taking things away from your kids?" The property battles were very ugly. Trying to figure out who got what, that made it quite bad.

Hurtful comments made by one parent about the other parent have a way of being taken personally by the children. It is not possible to always know how a child will hear such remarks, which is another good reason to keep these types of criticisms to oneself.

Loretta, 21 Dad was saying things like "I never, ever loved your mother. I don't know why I didn't get out of this sooner." I know he was saying those things to my brothers, and that was really painful, because it was like he was saying, "I wish you'd never been born." That was the implication behind that.

It's just really painful to think he never loved my mother. To think "Well, you loved my mother at some time, and you fell out of love" is one thing, but to think "You never loved her" is another thing entirely. I could always go, "When I was little, I know that wasn't true," but I don't know if my brothers have that same frame of reference, if they can think back, because I don't remember when it stopped. I don't know if they can think back and think, "My parents did love each other," and at least get reassurance in that.

Even when Barb reluctantly accepts the position of mediator, the payoff is only more stress.

Barb, 18 I begged both of them to get together in the same house, my mom's house, so that we could go over these financial aid forms together. My father was "No. Why do we have to do this together? Give me the parts that you don't know." I'm like, "It's much easier than making all these phone calls. Please just sit down and let's do this." And then there was arguing between them in Chinese, and then my dad left, and nothing was accomplished. I was okay, but I really wasn't. What are you gonna do? You're extremely frustrated, completely feeling that you're going out of your mind.

Tom, 12 If they asked me to take sides, there'd be a war. I couldn't even imagine them trying to make me take sides. If my parents were that stupid, I'd just say, "Forget it. I'll just stay on the sidelines watching, and you have to go do whatever you do."

Six

CUSTODY AND CUSTODY WARS: Where Are We Going?

Custody takes several forms. There is legal custody, as in "joint legal custody," where parents are expected to cooperate on major decisions for their children. There is "sole legal custody," where one parent is responsible for making the decisions. Then there is physical custody, which most people would define as "where the child lives."

Many court systems have recognized that families and children are poorly served by these terms and have made changes to create labels that do not imply ownership of children or that one parent is the "real" parent while the other is the "visiting" parent.

It is crucial that parents do everything they can to resolve all custody issues amicably and that they continue to make adjustments as the children go through their developmental milestones and have different needs. If parents are having a difficult time either making these initial arrangements or making changes in the years that follow, then they should seek a form of dispute resolution, such as mediation.

When a dispute stems from a parent's genuine concern about the welfare of a child, the fear and desperation can be overwhelming for the parent, especially if a parent feels that the child is in danger of being harmed by the other parent. Like a bear that finds its cub surrounded by hunters, their shotguns cocked and aimed, a parent may react with panic, irrationality, and a rabid sense of protectiveness. Unfortunately, not all custody or visitation disputes arise from such genuine concern. They also arise from bitter

65

grudges and grievances that may have nothing to do with the children.

Even more difficult can be the parent who is emotionally scarred by traumatic family events in his or her own childhood; the parent's fears may resurface in the crisis of the failed marriage.

In these situations one expression commonly applies: "The children are being treated like pawns." I must say, though, that I have seen chess players give more thought to the loss of a pawn than many parents give to their children when they are in divorce disputes. In these cases a child becomes the weapon used by the parents to fight their personal war.

Taking the case to court should be seen as a last resort, because few processes are as destructive to children as a custody fight. Not only can the fight itself be a terrible ordeal, but the aftermath, in the form of postwar bitterness and hostility on the part of both the "winning" and "losing" parent, can last a lifetime. The children are caught in the middle, and usually nobody loses more than the children.

Joy, 14 We knew we might have to be part of the trial. It ended up that we didn't, but I remember for a long time I felt sick a lot, like I might throw up. I was scared. I thought that no matter what happened, someone was going to hate me. I thought maybe my brother and sisters and I would live in different places. I once heard my mom on the phone saying to my grandma that she wanted to get as far away from Dad as possible. So I thought we'd end up living far away and never seeing Dad again or maybe not see Mom again. I hated it. My brother and sisters and I have never talked about it. We never talked about it then, either. I talk about it with my social worker.

Riza, 18 I lived with my dad and visited Mom twice a year. And now, the past four years when I've been living with my mom, I went back to Dad's twice a year. It was just part of that written contract thing. I love that contract. It was the contract of my life. When I turned eighteen, I had to figure out when I wanted to see my dad and who pays for flights and stuff like that. It's like, "The contract over my life is over."

Roberta, 16 My brother moved in with my father in fifth grade. My brother had a lot of problems, and I don't blame him. He was living with me and my mom, and you can go nuts after a while. They decided it would be good if he moved out and lived with Dad for a while.

He was miserable there at first because Dad is virtually never home. He works such crazy hours and stuff, and he wasn't used to that. It had always been him and me together, and someone was always living with us, my grandmother or my uncle, and my mom's friends were in and out. People were at our house all the time, and my brother just wasn't used to being alone.

At the same time, moving down there started for him a relationship with my dad, and so whenever we went back to visit, he and Dad could pick up from wherever they left off. But Dad and I never had an actual start. I never lived with him, at least not since I was very young, so he never got to hang out with me on a daily basis to see what I'm actually like in the morning.

And they're guys! "Ooo, cars, ooo." You know? But when I tell him that I need sanitary napkins, he doesn't know what to do. He goes, "What? Hmmm? Huh?" And he's really into biking and all this stuff. I try to be into it, but I think it's real fake when you fake interest, you know what I mean?

Stephen, 7 I feel pushed around by everyone with this custody stuff. Nobody cares what I want. They just care what they want.

Martin, 18 My parents were very quiet about the divorce, including the custody thing. They didn't make us go into court with them. It was all on the side, away from the kids, while we were at school or something, so we weren't bothered by it.

Elliot, 11 Mom and Dad were acting like very little children fighting over a toy that you need to share sometimes. They weren't acting like kids who knew how to share. They were acting like kids who wanted to play with the toys all the time. And then with visitations or whatever, going from destination to destination, that would be like one of the kids just taking the toys and going to the corner and getting it by itself. That's the way they acted in the first few years of the divorce.

Nick, 17 Me and my dad get along great. We have a couple of hobbies that we both like to do. We joke around a lot. I think it's a lot stronger now because we see each other on a day-to-day basis, and it's not for a weekend or two weeks at a time.

And my relationship with my mom has really improved, too, because I didn't talk to her for months. I was kind of pissed off when she kicked me out, and I really didn't understand it. There was one time in the summer when I didn't come home 'cause I was just real messed up. She wanted me to go into a drug rehab place, and I was like, "Okay, I'll go down and see it," but when I got down there, I decided all those people were really screwed up, and I felt I didn't have to be there, so I just made up some story so it wouldn't seem like I had to be there. I was under the impression that the woman there wasn't gonna tell anyone, but she told my psychiatrist guy, and he told my mom, and my mom got real pissed off that I was lying to her.

I think that that's one of the main reasons she kicked me out, and also for me to get a job. I just never got along with my mom, especially as I got older. She seems to think I blame her for the divorce. If it is, it's subconscious. I don't even think it's that. I've never gotten the whole story on it, how they split up. I heard something about an affair, but I don't know.

Jason, 13 The toughest part of my parents being divorced is living with my mom. I think it'd be easier with my dad living here, because then I'd see him more, and I'd have more of a male influence. Plus, my mom's more strict, because her mother was mean. She really didn't have a childhood. When she was younger, like in fifth grade, she was a tomboy. So I can relate to some of that stuff. And she used to play softball. She quit last year. So I can relate to that. But otherwise she's a lot more strict than my dad is. I kind of want to live with my dad.

But I think he'd be a little bit more strict than he is now, you know. He doesn't have to worry about me as much, like about schoolwork and my curfew and stuff. On a school night, with my mom, my curfew's seven o'clock. With my dad I have a feeling he'd let me stay out till nine or nine-thirty, because he's a lot nicer about that. I think it'd be easier with him. But what I'd really like is my mom and dad to switch places. I want to live here where my friends are and stuff. At his apartment there are no friends.

Ted, 12 My dad told the judge that it would be better for me to live with my mom. He was right, probably. It would be weird living all the time at my dad's. I'd have a lot more chores to do.

April, 12 If I had three wishes, the first one would be to be thin, because my parents fight about how much I eat. I heard my dad yelling at my mom once that if she got custody, I'd turn into a fat pig just like her.

Shanon, 10 My dad lost the custody fight, and I hardly ever see him now. I still can't figure out why he wanted me to live over there.

Nicole, 19 The day we moved out, my father and I went for a ride, talking, and he said that he felt we should stay with my mom, that she should have custody, and that he knew how close we were with her. So, as hard as it was to hear him say that—"Well, you're only going to have main custody with one of us"—it was also what we wanted, because we both knew that my mom was the one we'd want to stay with. My dad worked long hours, and my mom was the one who had always done the house stuff and the one we went to with all our questions and our school stuff, even though she had a job, too. She set it up so that she worked only the time that we were in school. Her schedule was more fit to be a parent.

But then it got crazy. A couple of months into the separation, my father's lawyer told him that the house usually goes with the parent who gets custody. My dad had always liked the house and the dog and everything, so he decided to fight for custody—after he had told us that he knew he wouldn't be as good a single parent as my mom would.

That was difficult. All of a sudden everything was thrown up in the air again, and that was really hard for my mom, because she knew that he made more money and that he would be more financially stable. She was afraid things like that might set it off in the court so that he'd get custody, and even he admitted we would be better off with her.

Jamal, 20 I always go with my mom. My brother, he would try to stay with my dad sometimes. It didn't work out, but for a long time I didn't see them.

Barb, 18 All of my life until maybe the last year there have always been family fights. There was so much turmoil at my mother's house and so much stress, and there was yelling and verbal and some physical— I wouldn't say abuse, but things that hurt you very much. I couldn't take it any longer, and luckily enough, my dad had moved, and he bought a home in order to be closer to us kids, more accessible.

And one day when I came home, I took my bags and left, crying. I couldn't take it any longer. I went to my dad's. I was repeatedly kicked out of the house by my mother or told in anger to get out of the house or to "go to your dad's where you're wanted." But when you ask her about it nowadays, she says, "You know, I don't remember this, because it's just things said in anger that you just don't realize." And so I have stayed two summers so far with my dad.

Hank, 8 Dad's a real good cook. Mom likes to take us to Toys-R-Us. I don't see why things can't stay okay, why they have to fight.

Charlene, 6 Dad likes tickling me, and I like it, but Mom doesn't. She says she doesn't trust him.

Richard, 15 I hear one story from my mother and one story from my father. My mother tells me that she's fighting for custody because Dad drinks and she doesn't want me growing up in an alcoholic household. I'm fifteen, man. If she was so worried about me not growing up in an alcoholic household, why didn't she get a divorce a long time ago? My dad tells me that he hardly drinks anymore because he doesn't have to now that he doesn't have to listen to "her" anymore. He says that he's fighting for custody because he doesn't want me living with someone with her morals at a time in my life where I'm learning about becoming an adult. Same thing with him—if her morals are so bad, why did he stay all those years? He's mad because she has a boyfriend, supposedly. I've never seen the guy, and I don't want to. So then Mom tells me that he had one-night stands for years when he was drunk. I just can't wait until I'm old enough to move out, and then I won't have to listen to any of it. If they start, I'll just tell them to drop dead, and I'll go home to my place. I don't feel like I have any place right now. I just wish they'd both just shut up.

Ken, 13 It was good that they settled all the custody stuff themselves instead of lawyers.

Even if the impulse is to get as far away from each other as possible, parents make things much easier on the children if they can arrange to live reasonably close together.

Jamal, 20 He left the house, and we stayed. My father bought a house less than a mile away. It was around the corner but a totally different neighborhood, totally different town. But I could still ride my bike there, and I rode my bike over there a lot. He never moved that far away, and when she sold the house, he sold his house, and now they're still less than fifteen minutes apart.

Nicole, 19 With the custody fight I guess it was just a few months before my dad finally realized that it was crazy. Actually, my parents knew most of the judges just because they both lived in the area for years. My dad's lived there since he was two. They know everybody in the community, so one of the judges just said, "Hey, look, this is ridiculous." And I guess it finally evolved that he would quit or that it wasn't working out or something. We weren't pulled into it as much as a lot of my friends have been who have gone through things like this. The way that we were pulled in was just people saying to us, "What do you think? Would you be okay living with your dad?" And we didn't want to say, "No, I want to live with my mom," but we didn't want to say, "Well yeah, that would be fine," because then it was going to be difficult either way.

We didn't end up having to testify in court, although they thought we were going to have to. That was scary—the idea of having to do that—because I didn't want to jeopardize anything with my dad, but I knew that for main custody, for the person that I would want to actually live with, that I'd want to stay with my mom. But that didn't mean that I had anything against my dad. That would have been difficult, to have to say, "I don't want to live with you, Dad," when I knew that that would probably make things difficult between the two of us.

April, 12 I'm totally caught in the middle. Why do they all care what I think? I wish they'd just leave me alone.

In anger, parents will sometimes say exactly the wrong thing. What Max heard confirmed his worst fears.

Max, 9 My mother told me that when she gets custody, I'll never see Dad again. Or maybe she says he'll never see me again. I guess it's the same thing.

Sometimes a malevolent custody fight can have tragic consequences.

Larry, 14 My brother ran away last year. He's sixteen, and we ain't seen him since Christmas Eve when my dad came to pick us up and they started fighting about what happened last time they were in court. So my mom slapped my dad, and Dad hit her back in the face hard with his fist, and Mom fell off the porch, and her nose was bleeding and everything. My brother ran in the house to call the police, and my dad ran and grabbed him and tore the phone off the wall. I ran into my room and started screaming and crying that I wanted to die and never see them again. Dad finally left, and in the middle of the night my brother ran away. So after five months nobody knows where my brother is. Do you believe they're still fighting for custody of me and him?

Nicole, 19 It works out well how it is, because my mom has custody. She's the one who really takes care of everything around the house. But then my dad and I get to go out and have fun, and he and I have always had more of the relationship where we have the same sense of humor and we like to do the same sorts of things for fun. Go-cart racing, boating, things like that have always been really more quality time with him. That made it nice in that there is joint custody but Mom has the main custody.

April, 12 If I had three wishes, I'd wish for Mom and Dad to stop arguing, for there to be no fighting in the world, and for my parents to stop going to court. The same thing always happens. They don't even have to tell me that another court date is coming because the weekend before, Dad gets real quiet when I'm with him, and Mom is in a bad mood the whole week. Then after the court date, they both cut each other down, and I hear them saying real bad stuff on the phone, and I hear Dad crying. Maybe I should make all three wishes be that Mom and Dad stop going to court dates.

Jackie, 9 I wish there were two of me so each of us could live with Mom and with Dad. But I'd hate it if there were two of my sister!

Amber, 7 Mom and Dad are both good to me, but they aren't good to each other. I guess I'm lucky that they're good to me.

Dexter, 13 I used to think it could never be as bad as it was when they would fight all the time. But even though we don't live all together now, it's worse because it's like they still fight, but now they say the stuff they used to say to us instead.

Drew, 6 I like it at Dad's. He has a lot more stuff, and I can get anything I want over there.

Robert, 13 When my parents fought for custody of me and my little brother, it was the scariest thing in the world, and it made me realize that marriage is stupid and having kids is something I'll never, ever do.

Nicole, 19 I guess there were always questions about privacy. I'm not really sure—things come out so much later on. I've learned a lot of things that happened, or I've been told happened, during their custody problems that I didn't know about at the time. I guess there was spying. My dad hired a spy, someone to spy on my mom, I guess. They were watching the house when we were there, and that was just really strange, the idea of that.

Stephen, 7 If I had three wishes, I'd like to be a cop, I'd like to have a machine gun, and I'd like to have a nuclear bomb. I'd show them how to fight a war.

My grandmother tells me that I should feel lucky that my mom cares enough to fight in court for me, but it all just makes me mad, like I want to kill everyone.

Terence, 11 If I have to go back to live with Mom, I'll run away or I'll kill myself, and I'll tell that to the judge when I get a chance.

Roberta, 16 I guess at one point they were going to get back together. He ended up getting transferred to Louisiana with the Marines, and so they did the whole custody thing. You know, Wednesday night at his house. Eat fish sticks. We would watch *The A-Team,* and he taught us how to knit. And I still knit sometimes. It's relaxing. And he taught my brother how, but he never really got into it. Mainly, we'd just go and chill over there, and every once in a while we'd stay the night over there.

Spencer, 16 What cracks me up is that Dad got custody of me, and his big thing was that there weren't as many gangs where he lived. But I was already in a gang near his apartment by the time they started fighting about custody, and I was never in one around our old house where Mom lived. What idiots. They didn't even know. They know now, but not back then.

George, 9 Mom lets me have pizza a lot, but don't tell Dad I said that, because he thinks I'll be fat like her. If I live with him, I'll probably never have pizza again.

Frank, 17 When they were fighting over us, I told the lawyer that I wanted to live with Dad, but I don't think I told him why. I remember feeling really sorry for Dad because he was going to be living all alone. I was only six, and the scariest thought in the world was being alone in a house. So I figured I'd have to live with Dad so he wouldn't have to be alone.

April, 12 I get along fine with both of them, and they don't talk about each other to me. But I know that soon I'll have to tell someone who I want to live with. It gives me bad dreams. Sometimes I can't sleep at all because I keep thinking about it.

Nick, 17 I graduated from high school last year, and I wasn't doing anything, just getting into trouble. I got arrested a couple of times just for stupid stuff, like breaking windows. And I tried to throw a beer bottle at some guy, so I got arrested for that. Little stuff. And then my mom kicked me out of the house. I moved in with a friend and his family.

I was living with them, and I didn't have a job, so I figured it was best that I go visit my dad. It was just for vacation, and I was gonna come back up. But I ended up staying because I got a really nice job down there. I miss being up here a lot, but I think I should stay where I am right now, because I don't wanna get in too much trouble.

Peter, 11 Ever since the custody fighting started, Dad actually tape-records some of what I say. I hate it. He says he's doing it for me.

Sheena, 5 Dad wants me to live with him and my stepmom, but I can't because she brushes my hair wrong. I have to stay with my mom because she brushes my hair the right way.

Peter, 11 I saw Dad hit Mom a lot, but because of that, Mom thinks I should never be able to see him. And so because of that, Dad thinks I should live with him. I don't care what happens.

Nick, 17 I think I've had one of the better divorces, because my mom and dad always seem to keep me and my sister in mind when they're making decisions. During fifth grade my mom and I really started fighting, so I moved in with my dad. I just always got along better with my dad. When I lived with him, he was more like "This is the way it's gonna be." My mom's kind of lax about everything, and she knew that I was really screwing up in school. I'm not gonna lie to myself about it, but I kind of lied to her. She always knew what was going on, but she just kind of let me do what I wanted to do. She would give me pointers or hints about what I should be doing, but I didn't listen to her. I think she's waiting for me to say, "I wish I had listened to you more."

Amber, 7 Mom has a super-big TV, so I guess that's where I'd like to live. But don't tell Dad I said that.

Charlene's fantasy is a common one.

Charlene, 6 I want to live with the richest parent so we can live in a big house, big enough that we can all live together again. So big that

Mom and Dad never have to see each other or fight, but we can all live there together.

Peter, 11 Don't tell my dad, but I really don't like his girlfriend or her kids. I pretended to, to make Dad happy. But now he thinks I should live there because he thinks I love them, and I don't even like them. I don't even know if I like my father anymore. But I still love him 'cause he's my father.

Parents often feel compelled to share their desire for custody with their children, but the result is usually that the child ends up feeling torn.

Joy, 14 I don't want to see my mother anymore. I don't want to visit with her, because she always tells me she wants me to live with her.

Andrew, 7 My sister and I used to get along great, but now we fight a lot. I think she should live with my mom, and I'll go with my dad. Mom and Dad can't get along, and neither can me and her, so it makes sense. Mom says the judge won't do that and that we should both live with her. But how does she know what the judge will say? She thought the other judge would say Dad should go to jail because he wouldn't give us all the money we should get, but she was wrong that time. I used to think she knew everything, but I know now that nobody really knows everything. But I think my dad knows more.

Justin, 8 Dad wants me to live with him, but he lives in an apartment building and we're the only kids there. I hate it there.

Jackie, 9 Dad keeps saying, "You'll get your own room." I used to care about that, but now I don't. I used to want to get away from my little brother, but now I don't. All I want is to keep our room and stay where we are. I don't know why everything had to get so bad. When I think about moving in with my dad and having my own room, all I want to do is cry.

Nick, 17 I don't like the way my mom is. She's like the feminist, and I don't think you can be a feminist around a teenage son who's gonna be dating whoever he wants and treating them like dirt. She was always giving me crap about that. I don't know, I'm more like my dad than I am like my mom, and my sister's just the opposite.

Barb, 18 Because they speak in Chinese and I don't speak Chinese or know Chinese, I don't know what they say when they speak to each other. All I know are the raised voices. All I know are the long pauses once in a while and the very angry voices. Now that I'm living with my dad, I hear my dad's side of the phone call. Before, I would always hear my hysterical mom yelling. Now I hear my dad's voice. It's not that I understand anything, I just hear it, which is a weird experience for me. It's very different. It's one of the— I wouldn't say perks, but it's one of the interesting things about living with my dad that I'm starting to see about him.

Cassandra, 19 I remember only once did I ever tell my mom, "Well, if this is the way it's going to be, I'm going to live with my dad." And I know that a lot of kids say, "I'll just go running to Dad," or Mom, or whatever. I only did that once, and I knew when I said it that there was no way I could ever live with him. I just wanted to see what my mother would do. I wanted to see what her reaction was. And she said, "Fine. Call him." And I was like, "Okay."

So I went and called him. I said something like "I want to come and visit you." And he was like, "Well, you're going to have to talk to your mom about that." Basically, he didn't want me to visit him. He's sixty-five, I think. And he still goes out and parties, and has all these girlfriends, and he says he doesn't want to grow up. He's just like he was when he was eighteen. He's Peter Pan. So that didn't work. And I knew it wouldn't work.

Riza, 18 The funny part is, the year that Dad finally got me to live with him was the year when I was just not ready to live with any parent whatsoever. It got kind of complex toward the end. We were all going to a psychologist. It was a big deal. Instead of saying, "Okay, she's just thirteen, and that's what happens when girls hit thirteen," we were all going into all these reasons, like "I miss my mother, and I won't accept the new family." And it had nothing to do with that. It was just the fact that I was thirteen.

The funniest part was that two and a half months before I left, it suddenly clicked. Suddenly I was friends with all of them. I remember one night at dinner we were all sitting there, and I wasn't rude anymore, and I didn't really hate everyone anymore. And we were all just kind of being peaceful, and that was the end of that. And for the next two months, for that summer, before I left, we were the closest family. And we still are.

Barb, 18 I have stayed two summers so far with my dad. I'm starting to get to know my father a little bit, which is kind of odd in itself in that I can honestly tell you I idolized him when I was a child. Now I'm starting to find the cracks, and it hurts. He's not this superdad that I thought he was. It's very painful, but I'm staying there for two reasons: One is to keep some sort of harmony. My brother stays with my mom, and they get along somewhat okay, or at least they can tolerate each other. I can't. Number two, to get to know my father better, because I didn't grow up with him, and if I saw him, it was maybe once or twice a month. We tried to make it a weekly thing, a Saturday or something like that, but it never really worked out. Someone's schedule was screwed up, either we had things to do on

Saturday or he had things to do on Saturday. Sometimes it ended up being once in two months. So you can imagine the kind of picture I had of my dad. I only saw him once in a while, and when I did see him, he was at his most friendliest and charming. My mom was kind of worried that he was going to be a Christmas daddy, but he didn't really give us gifts and stuff. He wasn't trying to bribe his way in.

Seven

VISITATION: Precious Time

Visitation is an outdated and inadequate word. In most situations a parent does not "visit," a parent parents.

How a mother and father divide their child's time between them should take the child's as well as the parents' circumstances and needs into account. As with custody, the child's development should be considered. For example, what makes sense for a five-year-old differs from what works best for a teen.

Parents should consider visitation sacred and protect it. Child support and visitation are unrelated issues, and parents must avoid thinking that child support buys visitation or that a lack of child support means a child has lost the right to spend time with a parent.

When many miles separate a parent and child, telephone contact can be an important way of keeping connected. It does not replace face-to-face time, but it can help maintain a relationship. It also allows the face-to-face time to start and end more smoothly, with less catching up required and farewells that do not truly mean "good-bye." Letters, e-mail, and home videotapes can also help bridge long distances.

Keep in mind that what matters most is not the amount of time one spends with one's child but how one uses that time.

Riza, 18 One of the things, surprisingly, that I like about growing up with divorced parents is that you get personal attention. The parents aren't distracted with each other. If they're not married or dating somebody else, you get absolute personal attention, and when my dad comes to visit me and the two of us go out to a park or something, it's just me and my dad. I was an only child. Now I have all these siblings. But for a really long time I was an only child, and it was great. It was just me and that parent.

Anne, 9 I picture my dad in my mind a lot. His face, his hairstyle. That's how I see him whenever I want, because he lives in Oregon and I can't see him for real very much. When I talk to him on the phone, I enjoy it, but it makes me sad. I feel a lot of different things mixed together. Sometimes it's easy to talk, and sometimes it's hard. We talk about all kinds of things, and it's kind of like talking to a friend.

Anger is a natural emotion for a child to feel when caught in a bad situation that he or she can't do anything to improve. Though it may be difficult to absorb this anger, it is important that a parent try not to take it personally even if the parent is on the receiving end of the fury. In many instances it is the parent to whom the child is closest that is the target of the rage, because the child feels secure enough in that relationship to let it all out, trusting that the bond will survive.

Robin, 19 I saw him once a month for the weekend, and I was always mad, so I would sit for the whole weekend and be mean. I was just sad and mad, and he knew I was mad, and he was mad back at me because we were so close. And then all of a sudden I was really mad at him, and he couldn't do anything about it, I guess.

This went on until recently. Now he's being a real dad. Like, we didn't talk to each other at all through my seventh-grade year, and then I saw him once in the eighth grade. Then he tried to start coming to things when I was in high school, but by then I was just like, "Get away." I was purposely rude. So then he didn't come anymore after that, and he was just like, "If you're not gonna respect me . . ." I was like, "I don't think you deserve it. You're being mean."

There are many books on the market for children of divorce. Not only can the content of these books be helpful for a child, but the parent and child can read them together and then discuss the ideas. This can be a good way for parents and children to enter into a subject area that might otherwise be tough to broach.

Tom, 12 Somebody gave me a book, it was *Dinosaurs Divorce*. It showed you all kinds of dinosaurs. I grew up with it. It showed what you could feel like or that you could be different, and it talked about feelings that your mother and father had, and so could you.

Loretta, 21 Maybe when kids are younger, it works better. Like my little stepsister. She seems to have two homes and seems to accept that. Two rooms, two homes, but my brothers and I didn't grow up with that. So I know my dad feels hurt. I think he felt like when he got divorced, he lost his kids because he lives somewhere else. But really, a lot of it is because of the way he treated people. But I think he blames it predominantly on just the moving out.

Elliot, 11 My dad wants to see us so much that he's trying to be nice to my mom. Now we see him either once a month or once every two weeks, but we used to be lucky if we saw him once every two months.

Cassandra, 19 My parents got divorced when I was two years old, and my memory of my dad is pretty limited because I was so young and because he lives in Tucson now, and he hardly ever comes to town. I haven't seen him for—oh, jeez—five years. We don't get along at all. In fact, we've been fighting now, and we haven't talked for almost a year.

Gretchen, 9 My dad lives in California now. He wants to be in the movies. We talk on the phone, and he tells me how beautiful it is there. I always ask him, "Did you get a part in a movie yet?" and he always says, "I'll call you when I get a part." I wish he would just come back here instead.

Roberta, 16 I'm leaving on Thursday for my dad's. We're going to spend spring break together, camping. We don't see each other that often, at most three times a year.

It's depressing to know that when I get on the train and come back, it's going to go back to what it is now, where I only talk to him every once in a while and we only see each other once in a while. I'll get really pissed off when I'm at school and girls are talking about their dads and what they do all the time. Sometimes I feel like I'm really gypped.

But then that's where my stepdad comes in. He and I are friends, and he's never gonna be the actual dad-thing. And I feel bad, and he feels bad because I do. Even though he met me when I was eight and now I'm sixteen, and he's known me for more than half of my life, he's never going to be "it." I need my own dad to say, "Hey, you know what, you are pretty cool," and be there. And my stepdad is totally there whenever I need him, no matter what. He tries and tries. He doesn't know what to do whenever I get off the phone with Dad, and I'm like, "What the hell just happened there?" He always feels bad even if I tell him I'm okay.

But when I'm with Dad, it's annoying, because we get along really good whenever we get beyond fake, uncomfortable, stupid stuff. He's a fun guy to hang out with. He's interesting, and he likes to goof off. He's not as serious as Mom is. She thinks the world's coming to an end, but Dad and I won't get into that. He's a fun guy to hang out with. But then it's just . . . I spent two really fun weeks with this great guy and then I'm going to be four hours away from him, and it's going to be like, "Hmmm. That's it."

Juan, 9 I started feeling low. I felt it. My dad, he couldn't go without my mom. He couldn't have a very nice house at first. He had a really screwed-up house. We have a better house now, but it's still not that good. He's saving up some money to buy a neater house. I didn't want to be with him because I'm allergic to fur. We were only renting that place. The owners had cats and dogs, and we stayed there for fourteen days, and it really got to me.

Cassandra, 19 My dad sends me birthday cards and Christmas cards and stuff, and in the last card he was like, "I wonder when I'm going to hear from you next." And sometimes I really want to call him, but then I know—it's been a cycle for years, on and off like this—and I know if I call him that it will just turn into another fight, and then we won't talk for a couple of months. And it's always me that has to call.

George, 9 I don't really care that much what we do when we get together, but I do wish we'd do more stuff. I get tired of just watching TV. But I'm glad we are together, so I'm not gonna complain.

Ted, 12 I like it in both homes, but I like being at my mom's when I'm sick. Dad's more fun when I'm not sick.

Though a detailed visitation plan is often an essential component to postseparation family life, parents also need to keep a child's development in mind. In this instance the fact that Ken is hitting adolescence means that he needs more flexibility in his scheduling than he might have at age ten, and this is not a bad thing. At this stage Ken's relationships with friends in his peer group are vital to his development. His parents have adjusted accordingly, which is not always easy because teens are not the most predictable people.

Ken, 13 Most of the time I see my father after school or on the weekends. He just stops by. If I call him and ask him if I can come over, Mom usually lets me stay with him. I called him up last Wednesday, and I told him that I was gonna be going uptown because we had only an hour of school. I wanted to walk around town and then go down to the beach, so I did that. And then we set it up for Friday. I wanted to hang around, since it was the first day off from school. So I did that, and then he called and said, "Do you want me to pick you up now before the Knicks game starts or after it's over?" So I said, "Afterward is fine." But then I got really bored, so I called him, and he came by and picked me up.

Riza, 18 My mom and I lived in Rome. Dad lived in a suburb of Rome for a while. And either I'd go to see him for the weekend or he'd come and see me over the week. Then my mom moved to Milan for three years.

So at age six I started taking trains back and forth by myself. I got real independent real early. I took buses by myself, trains by myself. I took a plane by myself for the first time when I was five. I was here in the States, visiting relatives. Unaccompanied minors have to wear a patch. I did that so many times. It was like an adventure. I loved the independence, saying, "Okay, bye, Mom. I'm going on the train now." I'd wave to her from the window.

Charlotte, 18 I hardly see my dad, so I probably would just continue to not see him very often once they split. I might even see him more, because I would have to make a conscious effort. Whereas now, yes, we live in the same house, but he's not really around that often.

Paul, 9 I hate having some stuff here and some stuff at my mom's. I used to like having it all together before they separated, but I didn't realize how much I liked it at the time. I didn't appreciate it.

Marta, 19 He'll send the cards, and he'll just write something like "Your dad always" or "I wonder when I'm going to hear from you next." But he won't ever write anything or tell me anything about his life.

Anne, 9 After the trip to see my father, my mom made a picture book from all the pictures I took. I don't miss him because I just feel sad when I miss him. So I don't miss him.

Roberta, 16 I don't know Dad. I don't know any of his childhood stories, like I do with my mom. I think he told me that he played a lot of college football, and he was really good, but he hurt his knees. I know little things he's interested in, that he does, that he likes. Before, I found out more from his mom than I knew from him. But I don't really know him that well.

Sally, 6 I don't see Dad that much because he's not making very much money. I miss him. He always calls us. We talk about school.

Riza, 18 My dad and I were really close for a while. He got this little apartment. I had kind of like a bunk bed, but it didn't have another bed underneath. There was a desk right underneath. I remember going to sleep with him working underneath at his computer, and it was really nice. We'd eat lunch together, and breakfast. That was probably our closest time.

Eight

PARENTIFICATION: Too Much, Too Soon

Simply put, parentified children are children who have had too much responsibility heaped on their shoulders. These often are children who are a delight to be around, the kids who seem older than their years, so polite, so helpful, so bright. They typically get approval for being this way not just from the family but from society. They also pay a huge price: their childhood.

Many of these kids have grown accustomed to helping a parent through tough times. Of course, there is nothing wrong with a child's being supportive. The trouble comes when the parent grows to rely on that support from the child. By then the roles have reversed to some degree, with the child parenting the parent.

Children who come from troubled homes are susceptible to parentification. For example, if a father cannot be counted on to support the mother, the mother may turn to a child for that support. This can be extremely seductive for the child, who might enjoy being the one who rescues Mom or Dad. With divorce come the perfect circumstances for parentification. One or both parents may be very needy, and the child, searching for some way to stay connected during this uncertain time, tries to help in any way he can. Add to that a child who feels guilty that he contributed to the failed marriage, and the urge to save Mom or Dad can become overwhelming.

For these reasons it is critical that parents find a support system during and after divorce. Be it a support group, individual therapy, counseling, involvement in church, or help *from adult friends or family members, parents must find ways to take care of themselves so that the children do not feel as if they must take care of their parents.*

Christina, 19 In some ways you have to play the parent, and I haven't really enjoyed that. You have to be there for your mom. When my mom is upset, we have to talk a lot. I have to cure all my mom's money worries. I get to worry about my mom's financial situation more than anybody else. I mean, Mom had to be both parents, and that's hard. And it's hard for me. I compare myself with other people, and nobody else has to do this. Nobody else has to listen to their mom crying about this stuff. But I don't have to call my dad and listen to his crap, either, so there are two sides to it.

Jewel, 18 Dad, he's like, "You should talk to your family," and I said, "You should reconsider the definition of family." They're the adults, I'm the kid. It's not my job to keep the family together. I've had to grow up enough. I'm not gonna be the matriarch of this family. So last year my father's sister called and wished me a happy birthday two weeks after my birthday. They don't even know when my birthday is.

Barb's situation is a perfect example of true parentification. She feels responsible not only for her parents' happiness but for the success or failure of her brother. In essence, Barb has been handed the reins of the family.

Barb, 18 My mom has often talked to me about my brother's difficulties in school and asked me for advice about tons of things. Like my dad would ask me about talking with my mom, how to approach her, stuff like that. One thing that I kind of complained about when I was crying one time my freshman year to a friend was a realization that I can't raise my brother. It hit me in college: "I am only one and a half years older than him, and if I knew how to raise my brother, I would." I'll be the most wonderful student, the world's most wonderful daughter, but I'm not a parent, and I just don't wanna be a parent.

My parents love me so much that they listen really hard to what I say, and they will take to heart what I'm saying. More likely than not, they will take my suggested course of action. And it's not that I would say, "Well, I really think that we need a new car now." It's stuff like "Okay, my brother's having difficulties in school. I think it's important that he sees the counselor at school so that she can advise as to how to deal with the teachers. I think that maybe we should consider a tutor" and stuff like that. "I really think also that he should see his father a little bit more. I don't feel that he and Dad get along very well. I think that he should live with Dad for a couple of years and see how it is." And Dad was like, "Yeah, that's a good idea. Let's have him stay at my place." This power, it's really, really weird.

Riza presents an interesting contrast to Barb. In Barb's family her parents explicitly look to her to take control whether or not she is comfortable with the burden. In Riza's case it appears to be her natural inclination to look past her own needs and shift into the position of nurturer. Though she enjoys that role, it is important for parents to find other, more age-appropriate roles for their children to fulfill. Remember that it is the children who are most in need of succor at this time.

Riza, 18 My immediate instinct in anything like this, not only with my parents but with my friends and anybody I know who is going through something really difficult, is to forget anything that I'm feeling and then completely go into caregiver mode. I'd make my dad lunch. I'd sit around and talk to him. I still haven't had a reaction to the whole thing. I react to it most strongly because of the way it affected my dad and not so much the way it affected me. I just completely pushed it out of my mind. I don't know that it's even there. If it is, and someday it erupts, then I'll find out.

I liked it because I felt like I could give back a little bit. I was eleven or twelve. Being the independent person I always was, I liked being able to go out and go shopping for us and help my dad get his little apartment together, move things in. It was a great moment of closeness for all the stuff that was going on then. I remember that time with fondness. It was just really nice to be that close to my dad and just share all this time, just the two of us. It's like the times before my mom was remarried when just the two of us would sit around and make pancakes on Saturday morning.

Fred, 9 My favorite thing about Dad is that he is understanding, and he really understands how I feel, but sometimes it is like I'm the father, because his feelings get hurt. Sometimes people tease my dad a lot. They hurt his feelings a lot. Sometimes he handles things by hurting other people's feelings with his fists. In a way, I don't blame him, because sometimes people are not nice to him. They call him and say, "I don't want you to work for me anymore" and use bad language against him. Those are the people that don't care about other people's feelings.

Barb, 18 My mother said, "Barb doesn't want me to date, and I love Barb so much, I will not do this." You see, it's a love that's very strong, and it's a power that can be extremely stressful and very scary. I'm only fourteen, I'm only fifteen, I'm only sixteen, and yet I'm making these major decisions. And it's happening. It's not like it's a figment of my imagination. They listen to me. So that was very, very weird.

I've gotten better at explaining this to people. I used to try to explain it as "too much love" or something, but that's not it. That's just a wrong description, and it doesn't explain anything. But there's some sort of power there that I have, that I'm afraid of, and that I don't know what to do with.

Nine

HOLIDAYS AND BIRTHDAYS: Precious Memories

Typically, holidays are about tradition, family, and memories, and all three are at stake during divorce. Many traditions are shattered when a marriage explodes. Holidays that children once looked forward to can become dates of dread if parents allow hostilities to interfere. If possible, holidays should be arranged months if not years ahead of time and without involving the children in the decisions. Holiday schedules that feature some sort of equitable split, whether by alternating year to year or with each parent taking certain holidays every year, allow for families to start new traditions. Such scheduling also allows children to look forward to an approaching holiday with excitement or at least with less apprehension.

Nicole, 19 Holidays have always been a stretch, especially right at the beginning. Being there at Christmas Eve, opening up the stockings with my dad's side of the family, knowing that my mom had one before. "Where's the stocking that has my mom's name on it? Did they just put it back in the box this year?"

Cassandra, 19 Holidays weren't difficult except for Easters. Twice, my father came during Easter. "Okay, I'm here. We're going to spend time together." This particular Easter I was so excited because I hadn't seen him for a couple of years. I told all my friends at church that my dad was going to come, and they'd get to meet him. He was actually staying with us, which was an interesting situation. I mean, he was on the couch, but it was still him and my mother under the same roof.

Easter morning I woke up and went out to the living room to see my dad and wake him up and everything, and my mom said, "Your dad's not here. He left. He went back to Tucson in the middle of the night." And I was like, "Oh!"

That was very traumatic for me. I was embarrassed because I'd have to tell my friends that my dad took off. I was hurt, and it was just terrible. When he finally called, my mom just laid into him. And since that time he's done it two more times. I think one of them might have been on Easter, but one of them was just another time around my birthday. "Okay, we're going to spend time together tomorrow." And he'll leave that night.

His excuse usually is "I ran out of money." No excuse at all. And then I gave him another chance and started writing to him and stuff like that, and calling. Christmases he'll usually try to send me a package of some clothes or a stereo or something. But I don't know where he picks this stuff up, but he has some pretty shady friends in Tucson on the pawnshop scene. The stuff that he usually gives me is secondhand. And while I appreciate that he has given thought in buying me stuff, I don't appreciate that almost everything he ever gives me is used. It just doesn't look nice or whatever. It is seedy.

Nicole, 19 All of a sudden, holidays took on a new feeling of "Oh, gosh, will there be tension? Will I have to be shuffled back and forth between the two parents all day? Will the family members make me feel awkward because I look more like my mom than I did last year? Will they make a joke about my dad at dinner?" Things like that play into it more just because it's a time when you expect to be with the whole family, including both of your parents. All of a sudden, when one of them is taken out, it adds a new dimension to the holiday, I guess.

Riza, 18 My birthdays alternated every year. I'd have birthday parties with my dad and birthday parties with my mom, and it just depended what year it was. Things like Passover, I'd either alternate, or it would depend on which family was having the bigger dinner, which one was more important for me to be at. I remember spending more holidays with my dad's family because they usually made a bigger deal. Birthdays, too. I mean, my mom would give me a present, and that would be my birthday. My dad is really into celebrating stuff. He really likes the whole hoopla around parties.

As a kid, I remember him planning the greatest parties for me. Like we had a pin-the-tail-on-the-donkey kind of thing where instead of a donkey it was Bugs Bunny. And he drew Bugs. He sat up all night copying Bugs on this big poster board. And he'd make these huge signs he'd always put on the door—"Happy Birthday, Riza"—and decorate them. And he'd have balloons all over the house. My dad always got into that stuff, so I remember spending more of the big holidays with him.

But I also remember spending holidays with my mom's family. It was just "Okay, I'm going with them this year." It was one of those things that was decided for me. The two of them came to a decision on where I'd spend the holiday and somebody would just tell me, and I'd say, "Okay." I felt fine either way.

Sally, 6 February is my favorite holiday because it is my birthday and because it is when my dad always comes into town for his convention.

Nicole, 19 A lot of the time, holidays are the main interaction I have with my dad's side of the family. Not just my dad but his entire side of the family. When I was sixteen, my dad and I got into a fight two days before Christmas Eve, and he ended up telling me he wasn't my father anymore, saying, "I disown you."

That was horribly difficult to handle on its own, and then on top of it I was not invited to the Christmas party anymore. For the first time, instead of going to the Christmas party, I ended up with my mom. It was so strange. All of a sudden, I wasn't invited, and my brother went because they were still on good terms. My dad had told us, "I don't have much money right now, so I'll give you each fifty dollars for Christmas, and then you can go get what you want."

So my brother went out with him, and he got two fifty-dollar bills instead of one. He got his present and my present, and I didn't even get a card or anything.

Then I got a letter from one of my aunts with a clipping out of the newspaper, Ann Landers or something, talking about how after the father died, this woman really wished that she had had a better relationship with her father. She wished she had said something before, and she knew that it was her fault. So my aunt sent me this card, saying, "Reconsider how you're acting toward your dad, and maybe you should say something to him." And I'm just like, "My father told me he disowned me and that I don't belong in the family anymore. I was not invited to the Christmas party anymore, and then everybody on that side all of a sudden thinks it's all my fault."

And it had all erupted because my dad said something I was doing was just like my mom, and then I made my little smart-mouthed response—"Thank you. I appreciate being called like my mother"—and he didn't like that at all, because he didn't mean it in a complimentary way. Then everything just exploded, and I have Dad's side of the family treating me the way they'd treated my mom a few years ago.

Tom, 12 Every other holiday I'm with my dad, and every other that I'm not with my dad, I'm with my mom. If I'm not with my mom on

Christmas, I'm with my mom on Easter, and with my dad, the same thing. After I got used to it, I liked the holidays. Before then I was saying, "Why couldn't I go to my mom?" when I was with my dad, and when I was with my mom, I would say, "Why can't I see my dad?"

Ken, 13 Christmas I spend with my dad. I sleep over Christmas Eve. In the morning I open presents and go over to my uncle's house. And then I spend the rest of the day with my mom. My birthday this year, I don't know what I'll do, because I'm turning fourteen. I might take a bunch of my friends waterskiing or something. It's more fun than sticking around here. But my other birthdays, I'd spend with my mom and my dad both.

What Barb describes here are the mental and emotional gymnastics parentified children often perform to take care of their parents. Though she has plenty of insight into how her own thoughts have worked under these conditions and is able to articulate these experiences beautifully, the concerns she feels are not unusual. Even when parents avoid putting their children in Barb's position of having to decide where she is most needed, children still worry about their parents. Barb's untenable struggle illustrates why the parents should be the ones who decide where a child goes for a holiday.

Barb, 18 Holidays were always a concern of mine. Like, "Who do I go to this holiday season? Who do I stay with?" And I picked it according to who I felt was feeling the loneliest. When my father was single, recently divorced again, I spent it with him first and then my mother even though my mother has been divorced and by herself all along. But I felt that my brother was there with her, and I should go to my father. When I felt that my mother was feeling lonely and she was all by herself, and that my father has friends and a family to go to, I went to my mother and stayed with her.

They were never authoritative in that sense. It's just odd. It was stressful, obviously. It was confusing, and it involved a lot of weighing of this and that, and trying to figure out who would feel hurt this season. You know? Who'd be alone sitting at the table eating rice alone? Who would that be this year? And crying—or if not crying, feeling very despondent and depressed. Who is it this year? Who is it this season?

Nicole's situation illustrates two different scenarios of handling holidays. For some holidays, her parents have been creative and have started new traditions, such as using the day after Thanksgiving as a new holiday. This type of alternating-holiday plan seems to work best for children, while the method her parents have used for Easter is an example of the type of setup many kids despise.

Nicole, 19 Holidays are always an interesting test of what's really going to happen after a divorce. In the divorce settlement, my parents were required to alternate holidays. So to this day we still alternate holidays, and Dad gets Thanksgiving and Mom gets Easter.

My mom has always been very good about following it. When it's my dad's holiday, it's my dad's holiday. On Thanksgiving we go with my dad, and we can be with him all day if we want to. On the day after Thanksgiving, Mom always makes a huge turkey dinner, and we have my grandma over and celebrate on our own.

When it comes to Easter, that's my mom's holiday. If our Easter party isn't until three in the afternoon, that really makes it difficult. Like this year it was at three, and I had church until noon. My dad wanted me to come over at twelve-thirty and stay until two forty-five so that I could spend some time with him. If I had just been able to stay with mom, been able to have our Easter baskets and spend the day with her, then spend the day before or the day after or something with Dad, it would have been a lot less difficult, but I don't think he realized that. When I tell him, he's like, "Oh, it's only a couple of hours. You can spend it with me."

That just makes us resent the tension between the two of them, where they can't give each other their own time. We're old enough now, I think, that we can make our own decisions about that.

Like with Christmas. Before the divorce we always had Christmas Eve with my dad's side and Christmas Day with my mom's side. After the divorce we just stuck with that. It was always difficult on a big holiday, though, knowing that if we were with my dad, my mom was home and what was she doing? Or if we were out with my mom, we were thinking, "Well, gosh, I wonder if dad's just sitting home." It was always like, "Can we go call him? Or will she think that's strange?"

Ken, 13 I celebrate Hanukkah and Christmas. My dad's Christian, my mom's Jewish, so I celebrate both. There are not as many Christian holidays as there are Jewish holidays. My aunt and uncle on my mom's side, they always do the Jewish holidays. I spend Easter with my dad. Valentine's Day, you don't really do anything, so it's not a big one. But actually I consider myself as having no religion. It's just easier.

Loretta, 21 Fortunately, this year the Christmas gathering on my mom's side was at my aunt's house, and my dad had his whole family over at his house, which is only three blocks away, so it wasn't a big deal to go back and forth. It's better than going back and forth between my mom's and dad's, but it still was a hassle. It was fragmented, back and forth, back and forth.

Christina, 19 It's weird now, especially because my father doesn't have anybody else, so there's much more of an obligation to do things with him during the holidays.

Roberta, 16 I try to go down to my dad's for Thanksgiving because Thanksgiving is food and it's fun. I also have all my relatives down there. Here we only have my grandmother, and my godparents live right down the road. But at my dad's, everyone's there. So that's very cool. We usually go down around Christmas, but Christmas is just not as much fun down there because they don't have little kids. And at their house, they climb out of bed at ten o'clock. We do presents, but they're like, "Ummm, yawn." And that's no fun.

Robin, 19 When I think of holidays, I have just general family strife feelings. It's always like that. I saw my dad for half the day on holidays, and then my brothers and sisters would come to our house for the other half of the day.

Tom, 12 We had holiday pageants, and my dad would sit on one end of the assembly hall, and my mom would sit on the other, looking at me, and I'm like, "Why do we have to be like this? Why are they separated, so far apart?" They were married for ten years or something like that, and why is it like this now?

Sonja, 15 Things were always confusing, because he would have to be careful how much time we spent together because of my mom. On Valentine's Day, when I was just a little kid, we were hoping my dad was gonna come and take us out. He ended up sending me a card saying "presents instead of presence."

So he ended up not coming around, because he wanted to give my mom space or whatever. So there was a two-month period where he'd call and send letters. We really didn't see him much, and that was strange, considering he was only fifteen or twenty minutes away.

Minnie, 14 Mother's Day is hard for me. My grandmother died on Mother's Day, which is part of it. I actually give a Mother's Day card to my dad. Do I give a card to my mom? I really don't want to. I hardly ever even see her. My sister and I always have to find a card that doesn't say, "To the World's Most Wonderful Mother," 'cause she's not. All the cards praise mothers. Well, you only give her credit for what contributions she made. My dad deserves a Mother's Day card, so I usually give him one. He's upset if he doesn't get one.

Nicole, 19 Before the divorce, my mom was always closer with Dad's side of the family than my dad was with his own family, and she was a big part of the holidays. My mom would hang out with them and do things with that family, so it was just so strange that all of a sudden she was out of the family completely. I have one aunt who will still ask about her, and a couple of cousins who do. When my dad's not around, when nobody else is around and it's just them, they'll say, "Is your mom doing okay?" The other ones basically pretend like I don't have a mother. I guess they're getting better about it now that I'm older, because I'll bring it up and not even worry about it. I've gotten to the point where, if they can't deal with it, that's their fault. I have a mother, and when they say, "So, what have you been doing?" I'm not going to pretend as if she isn't around or whatever.

My cousin on my mom's side of the family said to me one day, "Is he still my uncle? What do I call him if I see him?" And I had no idea. I said, "I'm going through this, too. I don't know." Things like that are hard.

Roberta, 16 Christmas is great, you know. You start out here, go to his place, his parents, her parents. Oh, it's awesome. My birthday? I love it. I get stuff from my stepgrandparents, my real grandparents, stepaunts and -uncles, real aunts and uncles. Definite advantages there. I wouldn't change it.

Winny, 12 For the last two years Dad comes here to town for holidays. We used to go there, but when I was nine and ten, I didn't really like it. Before that, the first one after the divorce, I wasn't really happy at first because it was the first one without my dad. Then the next one was okay, and now he comes here.

Nicole, 19 I think the easiest way to go about it is just to have it set so that you alternate holidays. Don't have it that you feel like you're torn, that you have to spend two hours with this person and then three hours with that person, and then go back to dinner with the other person. Just let the kids have a day. Let us have a whole holiday just with one parent.

I figure it's the meaning of the holiday, not the actual date. So if it's celebrated the day after Easter, you can still get into the mood of the holiday without it having to be on Sunday. God understands. Divorce happens.

Martin, 18 For holidays my dad came up, or we went down to where he lives. But there was never an increase in gifts—as the joke goes, "Oh, you get twice the gifts." Oh, yeah, that's great, except it's not true.

But my parents did seem to work out everything, including the whole "I'm getting him this." "Okay, that's fine. I'll get him the other."

Robin, 19 I didn't really enjoy holidays just because they were always a hassle, and I didn't really like going to Dad's anyway. He'd be like, "Here's your present," and I was like, "No, I don't deserve it. Take it back, 'cause I don't wanna be here very much." It was weird.

Christina, 19 Even though my dad has no contact with us, we always get a card from my grandmother, his mom. She has my birthday four days off and she misspells my name, but I totally don't mind. I told her how much it means that she remembers.

Nicole, 19 I really like holidays a lot now, more than I did at the beginning, right after the divorce and during the separation. Just the idea of "We're sitting here with Mom in the morning, and then Dad will come to take us away to the family party that Mom can't go to this year." It was always strange, the idea of "Dad is coming for a visit. Let's go out and get in the car with this person who just drove up, not somebody who lives here, and it's our dad." That was different.

Here is an example of how poor communication and heated emotions after a divorce can turn a holiday into a hellish memory.

Loretta, 21 I really thought I was through the worst part of my parents' divorce, and then Christmas came.

My fiancé, Edgar, surprised me and came to visit. That was the longest amount of time I'd spent at home since the divorce, and that's when I realized it wasn't settled, the whole thing with the holidays, who we were gonna spend which part of the holiday with. This whole tug-of-war thing was going on.

My dad was trying to cling to old traditions. My family was really big on traditions, and they had meaning. Like the Sunday after Thanksgiving, we would go to this Christmas tree farm, cut down a Christmas tree, and bring it back. We would eat crackers and little hot dogs, and spend all day decorating the tree together as a family.

I wasn't there for Thanksgiving, but Dad wanted my brothers the Sunday after Thanksgiving to go to the same Christmas tree farm. And Dad wanted us on Christmas morning, which is when we always opened Christmas presents. And Mom felt it would be better if we all started new traditions, and she was annoyed with Dad for trying to follow the old because here she was, cut out of it.

I know Mom was really upset because she took the boys to a different Christmas tree farm on a different day to start a new tradition, and they had a terrible time. Then Dad came and took them to the old Christmas tree farm, with the apple cider, and they loved it and had a great time.

What we ended up doing is, my brothers and I decided that Christmas Eve was Dad's day, and we would just pretend that was

Christmas with Dad, and Christmas Day would be Christmas with Mom. Part of it was based on my mom's work schedule; she had to work Christmas Eve anyway, but not Christmas Day. We were gonna spend the night at my dad's the night before Christmas Eve so that we would get up in the morning and open presents. It would be the whole thing, only just a day earlier, because that was what he wanted.

We went over to Dad's, but he wasn't there that night because he had gone to a party with his girlfriend. I knew that he wasn't gonna be home when we got there, and we were just hanging out at his house, watching movies or whatever, but it was a really stressful situation. My younger brother, Jim, is the one who actually decided that we should go and spend the night at Dad's, and Dad had told him at that point, "Well, I'm going to this party," and Jim said, "That's okay." But I think my older brother, Hugh, and I were kind of under the illusion that, yeah, Dad was going to this party, but he wasn't going to be gone long and was gonna come back at, say, nine o'clock, or at the very least he would call us and say he was staying a little later.

He didn't call, didn't come. It was a bad situation because Hugh was bored and making everyone miserable. Edgar was playing chess with him for a while, but he was still bored. He wanted his Nintendo. And Jim went out and rented movies, but nobody liked the movies Jim rented. My brothers wanted to bring the dog over, so we did, but no one was watching the dog, and she has a bladder control problem. She's a real mess, so I was following the dog around, cleaning up her accidents everywhere and getting really irritated because I didn't want to bring the dog over to begin with.

Hugh was getting really upset, like, "Where is Dad? Why isn't Dad here?" He was getting really belligerent and angry, understandably. Numerous times we'd thought of going home because it was just terrible, and at that point he didn't even have any beds, so we were all going to be sleeping on the floor anyway.

So Dad finally comes home at, like, eleven o'clock, and by then

Hugh had gone to bed, and Jim was still trying to watch his movies. I think Edgar and I were reading.

I wanted to talk to Dad, to explain what was going on. I wasn't angry, and I didn't feel like I was being confrontational. I just wanted to say, "It's been kind of a rough evening, and it would have been nice if you'd been here." In some way I wanted to express that, and I remember thinking about what I wanted to say. I was thinking, "Now don't attack him." I was trying to phrase things in a way that wouldn't be confrontational, in a way that would just say, "I wanna talk to you. I'm not angry. I just wanna talk to you."

I said one sentence to my father, and he just erupted. He was freaking out, just totally in a rage. I have rarely seen him that angry, and I was completely shocked. This just slapped me in the face. He was absolutely furious.

So Jim's crying, the dog's barking, Dad blames it all on Hugh immediately and starts screaming about how Hugh's just a snot-nosed little brat and this is all Hugh's fault. Then he runs in the other room and wakes up Hugh. I tried to follow him and stop him from getting to Hugh, and in trying to get into the room where Hugh was, he slammed my fingers in the door.

From that point I don't remember anything. I mean, I feel like I was really completely insane. I've never felt that way before. Hugh was in this room with Dad, and I couldn't get to him. And Dad was insane. I mean, he just wasn't my dad. I didn't expect that reaction from him, and I felt that I triggered it, I set it off. Why did I think I could talk to someone who was irresponsible? I can't even remember half of what he said that night because by that time, I was out of it.

I started screaming, screaming and screaming and screaming. I lost all control. I couldn't walk, I couldn't do anything, and Edgar picked me up and took me outside. I was still just screaming, and he sat me in the snow. Then I was okay. He went back in and got all of our stuff and got my brothers, and he got the dog. We all went home, back to Mom's.

And that's when I really turned against Dad. I mean, up until then I was trying to be neutral and fair. "Well, Dad's doing some bad things to you, but it's gonna iron out." I felt like I was just trying to reach out to him, to talk to him, and this is how he reacted, this is what he did to my brothers. It was a horrible mess.

We went home, all upset, and Mom was really worried. I just felt like he didn't love me, and it hit me in the face then. All along I'd been thinking that he was going through a rough time with Mom but that deep down he still loved me, he still loved all of us. He was gonna go back to being Dad someday, and it was gonna be fine. But at that point I was like, "He just doesn't love me anymore. He doesn't love my mother, and he doesn't love me, either." It really hurt.

Since then I haven't wanted to talk to my dad. I still don't feel comfortable bringing anything up even if he appears very rational, because I just can't know what he's gonna do and what repercussions it may have on other people, on my brothers. When Edgar went in to get our stuff that night, he sort of patched things up with my dad and basically portrayed it as a misunderstanding, which in part it was. But for me, Dad's reaction was a real betrayal.

The next morning he called us. I really didn't want to go, but I talked to my brothers about it, and we decided that we would go together. So Dad was all wonderful. "All a big misunderstanding. I'm so sorry." But he never really got it. He still doesn't get it, that it was much more than that, that you just don't go calling Hugh a brat and play it off the next day as "Oh, well, it was a misunderstanding." Obviously, a lot of deeper issues were coming out.

Ten

SIBLINGS: We're All in It Together, Aren't We?

> Brothers and sisters can be the most immediate source of
> support for one another during divorce, but they can also find
> themselves in the position of having to take sides with different
> parents or even being separated by a custody decision that
> divides them between parents.
>
> Parents should not assume that siblings will take care of one
> another during divorce. It is terrific if they do, but it may be
> too much to expect that a brother and a sister who had
> previously spent most of their time fighting would all of a
> sudden transform into a mutual support team because Mom
> and Dad are splitting. Parents should be very cautious,
> however, about dividing siblings, especially when they are
> young. The shared experiences of sibling life carry into
> adulthood when even contentious siblings might become closer.
> If they grow up in different households, this common ground
> will be diminished.

Nicole, 19 I have a brother, three and a half years older. I think
that made it nice because he and I went through it together. I think he
might have had more of an idea about it than I did, although I think we
were both pretty clueless before it happened.

Nick, 17 My sister and I got real close as we got older, which is
great. I really miss her now that we're living with different parents. She

was always somebody to talk to. Like, "You wanna go get something to eat?" I always asked her to come out with me and my friends, but she wasn't really into what we were doing. She was always like the older sibling even though I'm the older one. She was always more responsible. She was always the one left in charge of my little brother and sister. She was always in control.

Robin's father gave her the choice of leaving her mother's home to live with him and her older siblings when he moved out. Having been very close to her father, Robin said no, hoping that her dad would not leave. In the end she was separated not only from her father but from her siblings as well.

Robin, 19 The separation pretty much changed my relationship with everyone because I was mad at everyone. I became a bitter child. I was mad at Dad, and I was mad at all my sibs because they left, too. And I was mad at my little sister, the one who stayed with me and my mom, because she didn't care. My little sister was five, and she was just like, "Let's go play at Dad's," and I was like, "No, that's not what it's about." So I didn't like her because we'd go to his house, and she'd be all happy. I didn't like Mom because I never really got along that well with Mom. I didn't like anyone.

Jamal, 20 I think the divorce might have made my sister more unstable than any of us because she was the middle kid and the only girl, and my father loved her, loved her hard, and expected too much from her. She never got a lecture from him. I think the divorce hurt her the most. She's not stable anywhere. Everybody in my family is spoiled except for my sister. She had a little too much responsibility.

Loretta, 21 When they told us they were getting divorced, I had a lot of trouble deciding whether I should come home from school or not because for a while I had been planning on visiting my boyfriend in Japan. I was kind of like, "Well, should I go home? Do I need to go home?" I decided to go to Japan, and I felt really guilty about that. It was kind of a selfish thing. I felt it might be better for me if I wasn't home, but at the same time I felt bad because I wasn't there for my brothers who had nowhere to go. I wish now I could have taken them with me or something, just while Mom and Dad were working things through, so that they wouldn't have had to be there. I know my little brother got pretty angry at me. He's the middle one, and he expected me to be there and to take care of things. Since I wasn't, he felt he had to do it. He felt I had left them just like Dad had.

I felt it was my responsibility to protect them and to be there for them, to try to shield them from some of it. I didn't know everything that was going on with Dad and Mom. I get angry at my brothers sometimes because they feel it was easy for me because I wasn't there, which it wasn't. In some ways it was harder, although I can't imagine what it was like to have been there. But I was getting it from both sides.

Elliot, 11 A year or two after the divorce, my mom started getting stressed out. It's bothersome. Sometimes my parents couldn't help me since they were so stressed. Then I had to do stuff on my own and ask for help from my older brother or sister. Having a brother and sister helps so much. Sometimes they explain things better because they aren't so stressed, and I can understand them.

Nicole, 19 Things were always confusing about what was going to turn out, and my brother and I were always kind of confused. He was at the age where he just wanted to let it happen, and he just wanted to stay as far away from it as possible. He kind of went off with his friends and tried not to deal with it much, whereas I was at the age where I wanted to know what was going on. I wanted to be told things. We were in different stages.

Jewel, 18 The person who was hurt the most in this entire situation was my brother. My brother never saw what a man should be.

I mean, my mother is a strong woman, and I'm not so sure that you have to have a male figure in your life. I think male or female is fine as long as they're strong and show you the right road to go down. But for some reason my mom couldn't get through to him, and I think maybe that's where gender works. I think maybe that's where it's important, because you can identify with that.

And my brother saw my father being lazy and saw my father eke out an existence because people gave it all to him, because he never really worked for anything. And I see those same traits in my brother now, and it makes me very angry because that is where the damage was done. My brother couldn't see how to get beyond it. I'll break down and be awful and say, "You are acting just like Dad," and he will cry and cry, and he'll say, "No, no," because *Dad* is such a horrible word.

Christina, 19 My sister was angry and felt she was doing everything in trying to make a relationship with my dad, where I had a chip on my shoulder.

Barb, 18 My brother got disenchanted with my dad once he stopped being Disneyland Dad. I can tell you in the beginning years of the separation, he took us out to dinner a lot, we went bowling a lot, we went to movies and stuff, and he would buy my brother things. I wasn't really interested in that. It was okay but it wasn't so important. My brother and I just totally lost touch when he moved in with Dad, and now I see my dad in order to get more acquainted with my brother. Or to get closer to my brother, I sometimes resort to those old tactics, kind of like, "Oh, Brian, I just got this new stereo. You have to come check it out" or "Do you wanna go buy this new CD?"

My brother was left out of the loop. All the arguments, all the stress of the divorce and everything, it was never put on him because he has asthma, and they figured the extra emotional stress would trigger some sort of attack. So it was mostly me that knew about everything. I really don't know how much he knows or how much he knew about the details. Even though he's only one and a half years younger, they always spoke to me and they always spoke through me.

Nicole, 19 My brother and I would talk about the divorce together to a certain degree. He and I have always been really close, so that made it nice to have my brother to go through it with. Seeing how he dealt with it was interesting, since we dealt with it so differently. I think he was confused about why I always wanted to talk about it. He just wanted to shove it under the carpet and just be done with it. I was confused by why he didn't want to bring it up and didn't want to talk about it as much. But I guess when things really got down to the wire, when there was something concerning us, I always felt I could chat with him about it. He was always the good brother. I'm sure it would have been a completely different process if I hadn't been going through it with him.

Jamal, 20 I've always had a relationship with everybody in the family, but my sister, brother, and I had more of a relationship. My brother helped me get through it. I mean, we just never thought about it. My brother did everything he could to take us places in his car, just went out of his way to do stuff for us. My brother really wouldn't trip out. He wouldn't say too much about it. Neither would my sister. She would just make little comments. We would know they were fighting, and we would all look at each other and look back down. A lot of times my sister and brother had to call the police because of the fighting.

Loretta, 21 My brother just doesn't talk, and I wonder if he's letting any of his feelings out. The only way he really lets his feelings out is to try to manipulate my parents all the time. At one point Hugh got real angry at Mom over something or other and said, "Well, that's it. I'm gonna go live with Dad," and she just absolutely hit the ceiling. "That isn't how you handle relationships. You're gonna stay here and you're gonna fight with me, and that's how it's gonna be."

Christina, 19 Strangely, I ended up very much stronger emotionally than my sister, Lucy. Sometimes I wonder if the fact that she was so tied to my father left her feeling much more abandoned when he left. Looking at other people, I'm like, "I don't have a dad, boo-hoo," but within myself I don't really have a sense that there's anything else I missed, because I don't remember him being there. That's really hard between us, because she is a lot closer to him and wants to be close to him. Mom feels that Lucy is more like my dad in personality. In a funny way, I think Mom was more like Lucy when she was younger, Mom is aware of this, and that's one way in which it's hard for her to deal with Lucy. And so I think Lucy has a lot less self-confidence than I do.

Parents can lose sight of how an action in favor of one child can be hurtful for the other. In Nicole's example it appears that her father was in fact deliberately striking back at his daughter through his son.

Nicole, 19 When my father and I had a falling out for a while, I think my brother always felt torn, because he was still getting along with my dad. When Christmas time came around, I told him, "Well, of course you can go to the Christmas party. Don't worry about it just because I'm not going to be there." But then he came home with both his present and mine—Dad gave him both for himself—and it was like, "Oh, okay." I think he had as hard a time with that as I did. He even mentions now that he had thought about giving it back or something, because he didn't want to have to come home and tell me, "Well, yeah, I got both of ours." He wanted to give me mine, and I said, "No, I don't want it. He gave it to you. You keep it. That's fine." I didn't want to hurt my brother because I was hurting about my dad. I really had a hard time with the idea that I was pulling him into it.

But my brother and I have always had a really cool relationship, so we could talk about things like that. I think my brother always had a hard time dealing with all of it. I think in addition to the divorce he probably feels torn between my mom and my dad, and then when my dad and I were having a hard time, he felt he was torn between my dad and me.

Jamal, 20 I had a lot of friends and relatives who had the situation where their fathers were never there. I had a mother and a father. When they were fighting, I had my big brother, and he would always straighten it out. I mean, not between them two, but for me and my sister. He would always take our mind off it.

Then there was my sister and me. We would fight like my parents fought. A day didn't go by when me and my sister didn't get into a knock-down-drag-out fight. Until I outgrew her, she used to kill me. She would just terrorize me. But I got taller, and then we just switched.

Robin, 19 Me and my sibs never talked about the divorce. Not really. My family's not very supportive or close, I guess. I wish it was. They all care, but . . . My little sister, she is very much like my mom, except she's not bad at sticking up for herself. If Mom yells at her, she'll yell right back, no hesitation. If they ever got to hitting, my little sister would just hit her right back. If I was the last one at home like she is, it would be better to be that way than to be like me.

Winny, 12 I do miss my dad, but I think my brother misses him more than I do. I don't think my brother likes living with girls.

Eleven

MOM AND DAD AND DATING AND SEX: Yuch!!!

Divorce means Mom and Dad will be single, and eventually
they will probably date. This is normal, of course, but it might
not seem so to the kids. Most children (and many adults, for
that matter) don't even like to imagine that Mom and Dad
had sex together, let alone the idea of Mom and Dad having
sex with other people.

And with dating comes the possibility that a new person
might become a new stepparent. To a child who is still growing
accustomed to the idea of Mom and Dad living apart, the
thought of a new person taking up Mom's or Dad's attention,
affection, time, and house space can be tough to swallow. For
pubescent and adolescent children who are grappling with their
own sexuality, not to mention hormones, having parents who
are rediscovering or redefining their own sexual identities can
make for a queasy combination.

Robin, 19 My father and his wife have this thing. I used to think
they did it just to make me mad, but they still do it, and I know
they're not trying to make me mad now. Maybe they just do it all the
time.

They kiss before they do all sorts of things. They kiss before they
start their car. They kiss before they start eating. It's like, "Stop. I don't
wanna see it. If I was here with a boyfriend, I wouldn't kiss in front of
you—at least not a lot." It's like their little ritual thing. Gag. I used to

think they did it just because I was around, and then I'd get really mad. They don't try to curb things at all.

Robin's feelings about her father's and stepmother's displays of affection are common. Riza's abiding reaction is less so. However, a new stage of development meant a new attitude, even for her.

Riza, 18 My dad's a really openly affectionate person. When he was dating, you could tell, especially with his second wife. They were really affectionate. I was seven, eight, nine, ten.

I didn't mind at all. Actually, that went right up to adolescence. I got uncomfortable as soon as I hit puberty, and I got really uncomfortable with nudity around the house. Like, I wouldn't undress before I went to the shower. I'd go into the shower with all my clothes and come out fully dressed. So that's when I got kind of uncomfortable around it. I was like, "Okay, that's my dad, that's my stepmom, and this is me."

Anthony, 13 My dad has a girlfriend. She's nice, and it's not like they go and get all romantic in front of me or anything like that. They hold hands, but it doesn't bother me that much. It's like seeing somebody hold hands in public, sort of like people that you don't know. She's an old high school friend that he had. He met her at his reunion. This was two years ago. It's pretty cool. She does some of the stuff that I like doing, like putting together puzzles. Right now she's working on a huge, two-thousand-piece puzzle.

As with any aspect of divorce, a parent can make things more tolerable by respecting a child's feelings. Loretta's mom was not afraid to ask her children for their reactions to her dating.

Loretta, 21 My mom started dating someone, and she's still dating him. She met him at work. He has a daughter, and he's been divorced about five years. His daughter's about nine. He's a really nice guy. We liked him because we can see that he treats Mom well, that he's a mature, responsible individual. I know my brothers have felt a little uncomfortable around him, but Mom has always tried to make them feel comfortable and has tried to say, "Do you mind if he comes over for this? Are you uncomfortable if I hold hands with him in front of you? Would you prefer that I didn't?" That kind of thing.

Winny, 12 My mom doesn't go out on dates. She goes out with my friend's mom and boyfriend. Or she goes to dances or whatever. She doesn't have a boyfriend. That would be bad if she did because I don't think I would like him. My friend's mom has a boyfriend, and he wants to marry her mom. Every time that her mom tells her that, she starts crying and running upstairs. He's really not all that mean, but she always says she hates him because she doesn't want her mom to marry him. I think I'd feel the same way if my mom had a boyfriend. I don't think Dad would have a girlfriend, because he's the one who really wants to get back together with my mom.

What might seem funny to a parent might not be funny to a child.

Cassandra, 19 Whenever my mom and stepdad-to-be would kiss or show any signs of intimacy, I'd be like, "Okay, guys, let's put the brakes on. Not in front of me, okay?" That was like a big deal, and then they'd do it to tease me sometimes, and it was just weird.

Nicole, 19 Both my mom and my dad have dated the parents of people in my grade at high school, and that was always strange. Neither of the kids my age were close friends of mine, so it was always strange when we'd walk by each other in the hall or wherever. One of them, his dad dated my mom for quite a while. It was strange when I'd see him at social gatherings, because his friends were kind of friends with my friends, but it wasn't like we hung out a lot. It was always awkward, like, "Oh, uh, hi." "Yeah, hi."

Ken, 13 My mom's sort of seeing somebody that she likes. He's really nice, so I like him. He's a little bit older than my mom, but I like him still. And he has kids, so I can relate. Or maybe it is more that he can relate. I mean, he knows how to act around kids. Somebody who has never had kids or experience with kids, they come up to you and they're doing some of the stuff that they like, but the kids don't. It's a lot better to have somebody who enjoys just seeing kids, like teachers.

Jamal, 20 Neither one of them ever married again, but my mom went out with a couple of guys. They were nice guys. We'd talk about sports. I could see she was going through a tough time. She needed some type of outlet. These were guys she liked. They would all play cards and stuff. It wasn't strange. I mean, with my father it was strange, because when I'd see him, he'd be with younger people.

Elliot, 11 I think it's normal that Mom and Dad go on dates with people since, I mean, it's the basic facts of life. You just have to go on with your life. You can't just stand in the same spot and go nowhere.

One of the fears that children have when their parents start to date is that they will lose that parent to the paramour or that their time with the parent will forever include the new love interest. There is never any reason for parents to force the issue of their single status on the children. The fact that Mom or Dad is in love in no way diminishes a child's need for one-on-one time with his parents.

Loretta, 21 My mom mentioned that she thought Dad had broken up with his girlfriend, but she didn't know anything else. Then he called me a couple of days later and said that she had left him. I think we all were pretty much overjoyed. He was very hurt, but we felt like,

"Maybe he's gonna be okay now. Maybe he's gonna pull himself together."

Throughout the summer while the divorce was going on, which was the summer after my sophomore year in college, right up until his girlfriend left him, he would call me and say things like "Well, you know I really am gonna try to work harder on my relationship with your brother, and I'm gonna fix things," and whatever. What made it so hard is that not only had he been acting completely irresponsibly, but he would try to act like he was changing.

So I would kind of pass these things on to Hugh, but then Dad would do something else. He was constantly trying to trick my brother into going places with him and his girlfriend. He bought four tickets to a big football game, and he didn't tell Hugh until the day they were leaving that she was coming along. So my brother didn't go, but he was very hurt because he'd been looking forward to this, just his dad and him. Then she was thrown into the picture.

At one point my dad was gonna drive up here, pick me up, and move me down to my summer internship. I was absolutely terrified he was gonna bring her up here with him, because I would have been so embarrassed. I just did not want him anywhere near my college friends with her around. I didn't want my college friends seeing him acting like that, with that bimbo. When I first came here, they thought I was a hick thing from Missouri, with my accent and whatnot, so I didn't want them thinking, "Oh, God, your dad, he's even more of a hick." I didn't want to be put in the position of having to defend him, but, fortunately, she didn't come along.

Christina, 19 My mom hates going to graduations and stuff like that because it's all these married couples and she's by herself.

Paul, 9 I think about a lot of things. I think about if my mom and her boyfriend will get married. I don't talk to her about it, but I think about it a lot.

Riza, 18 I don't actually remember when my mom and stepdad moved in together, but I do remember the before and the after. And I remember that I didn't like the fact that it wasn't just me and my mom anymore—not that I didn't have a bunch of problems when it was just me and my mom.

I was very angry at her cello. There was one night when I almost kicked a hole right through it because she was always at rehearsals or at concerts. I was a latchkey kid. I would come home from school and heat up my own lunch, watch TV, and do my own thing.

I had some problems with the fact that she didn't give me enough time as it was, and now she had him, and he was also in the orchestra. So she was gone, she was with him, and I was really alone now. It's not like it was just the cello taking her away, it was everything. I had a little bitterness about that.

Anne, 9 They divorced when I was in preschool. My dad had a friend who had a sailboat that he loved to sail in, and when I was old enough, he'd take me with him. After the divorce, when he lived here, I saw him once a week. Then one day he got a girlfriend. She was kind of nice, and they moved to Nevada. I hope he misses sailing as much as I miss him.

Barb, 18 I didn't want anybody in the house. I felt my personal space being invaded. I didn't want any more emotional stuff brought in this household that we were living in, you see? Dad was living somewhere else. He had his own space. I saw him once a week, twice a week. It was okay. I heard him say that he was going out and stuff. I didn't have a problem with that.

But at home, with my mom's friend, I did not want a new father figure. I started to recoil when he came. I suddenly developed a huge personal space. To this day people with the same mustache that he has, and the same general countenance and general physiognomy, just make me shiver, and I want to get away from them. I don't want them around. And it's horrible.

Ken, 13 I'm positive about this. I don't want Mom or Dad to get married. I don't care if they have, like, you know, boyfriends or girlfriends, but I just don't want them to get married. I know I don't want my mom to get married. My dad, I don't live with him, so I can't stop him.

I don't want another father that I don't know as much. If I don't like him and she marries him, it's kind of annoying having this guy who thinks he likes kids or knows what they like. Because then he's like, "Oh, let's go do something." He thinks he knows what you like, or he tries to make you laugh and stuff like that.

Same thing with my dad, because say I go over to his place and I see his girlfriend now. That's cool. But I just don't want to have two moms or have a stepmom and a mom. It's just easier having one parent or, actually, two parents. You don't have to worry about Mother's Day or Father's Day, getting two presents for fathers or two presents for mothers. You don't have to worry about birthdays, about them getting you something or doing something with you.

Jewel, 18 I was thirteen. That was around the time I was growing into my own person, starting to be faced with choices of having relationships with other people, and I saw my dad throwing his sexuality around, carrying on with these women all the time behind my mother's back. It's just so raunchy, it's just like, "You're so disgusting."

Nicole, 19 Little things they say that they don't know kids pick up on really stick with you. You go, "Oh, gosh, that's my dad," or, "That's my mom. What are they saying?" It's just something you have to deal with that you never would have thought of before. Oh, gosh, it's still strange to think about, and I'm a lot older now. It's different with my two parents because one of them is very moralistic and doesn't do much outside of marriage and things like that. So that's easy to handle.

But then the other one has said things to me before like "Yeah, I went and got HIV tested. It's the intelligent thing for a sexually active adult to do." And I'm just like, "Oh, no! Don't tell me that! Oh, God! I can't handle this."

They talk to me about things and say, "When I went over there the other night . . ." It's just strange to hear stories about it and think, "Those are my parents. They aren't supposed to be talking like that. They're supposed to be thinking about retirement plans or sitting home at night watching a movie together or something."

Riza, 18 My dad and his current wife actually met through a "friend service" thing, one of those completely confidential ones where you can call a number and leave a message, and then that person can screen all the calls and see if she wants to call anybody back. That's how they met, which to this very day weirds me out because it's like, "My Dad called up a phone dating service and met my stepmom!" Actually, there was some article in a paper bashing these services, so the two of them wrote this really terse letter: "We went through this, and we have this really happy family. We have all these kids. It works." But still to this day it weirds me out, the whole dating thing.

So she called him back, and they went out for dinner. My dad's not supposed to do that kind of dating. It's for a single guy who's a twenty-something kind of person. My dad wasn't twenty-something at that point. He had passed the thirty mark. He had been married a couple of times. He was supposed to meet people through friends.

Rodney, 18 When my dad and her would hold hands, it was a little weird at first, but when I saw how happy he was with her, then I thought, "Well, man, he never did this with my mom." It did make me feel good, like this is a good thing for him, and she's such a nice person. She's a lot like my mom in some ways, and in a lot of ways she's a lot better than my mom. She sort of looks like my mom, which kind of felt weird to me and which I found interesting. I never mentioned this to him. I'm sure he must know it, like, if he could have found anyone that looks like my mom, it would have been her.

Robin, 19 My friends always say that when their parents kiss, it grosses them out. I was just like, "Well, don't you think they did all of this stuff? Come on. You're here, aren't you?" But I never really thought about it, because my parents never did it when I was around. I'm not sure I thought about it at that point or not because I was only ten. I remember his girlfriend, and I was mad because I didn't like her. But I don't remember thinking anything else.

Roberta, 16 Craig, Mom's old boyfriend, and my mom, they had kind of broken up. As soon as Craig found out that Harry, my stepdad-to-be, was in the picture, Craig said, "Well, marry me." So my mom, my brother, and I, we sat around the kitchen table, and Mom said, "Okay, we marry Craig or we date Harry. What do you want to do?" And we said, "Craig's hitting the road. We hate the guy. Mom, you know we don't like him." We'd made that clear. She would go out on a date with some guy, and then on the second date she would bring him home, and we'd critique him. So she knew from the beginning that we didn't like him.

She was good. We would talk about things. She'd say, "Well, how come you don't like him?" And we would say something that we didn't like, and she would be like, "Well, I see this good thing in him. Maybe you're not giving him a chance." Or, "Yeah, that annoyed me, too." We would all sit around and talk about it. And it wouldn't be "Well, Joe, my kids don't like you. Good-bye." We would get to know the guy. It's not like she was some person who had a million guys. I can count three whose names I can still remember.

Harry had come over for dinner a couple of times. Otherwise, we wouldn't have said, "Date Harry." No, we had met him a couple of times. He was a cool guy. There was this place he brought us to called the Game Joint. They had ten thousand different games going on, and there was a back room, and they'd play pool there. Or basketball. I went there a couple of times.

Harry had taken us out a couple of times, and he had taken my brother to a barbecue and a couple of things here and there. He had gotten to know us. So as soon as Craig found out Harry was around, Craig came right back into the picture. "Oh, marry me, Gladys." And we said, "No, go away." So he went away.

So she started dating Harry with our blessing. Then my brother moved in with my dad, so then it was just us. And it was really cool. It was just the three of us who hung out all the time. One memory that I have is memorizing the times tables. He had worked out this whole big, long times-table thing so that, for example, when I got to the number three, he's like, "The number three buys you three circus tickets." So he went and bought me circus tickets, and the three of us went to the circus.

Loretta, 21 At first I felt like my mom's fiancé was totally trying to impress me, which I'm sure he was, and that made me uncomfortable. I was like, "You don't need to impress me. I like you, I think you're a nice guy, I think you treat my mom well, and that's all that really matters." That was really weird, the idea of someone who liked my mom trying to impress me.

Riza, 18 I never felt anything was a problem with my mom and her boyfriend. All three of us went out for pizza, and the two of them said, "We're going to get married." And I was like, "Oh, okay." You know, I just sort of accepted it. It was like my parents make these decisions, and "Isn't that nice." I was eleven. I remember not really knowing what to do with that information. "Oh, okay. Here we go again."

Cassandra, 19 Mom went on dates every now and then, but she didn't see anybody seriously, so it was really strange for me when she started getting more serious. When I was in fourth or fifth grade, she got together with an old friend of my dad's, and he obviously thought she was quite an item. And I was not thrilled with this at all. I was very, very angry, and I made it known. When I was a child, he would play with me and stuff, and we'd have a good time and whatever.

But this time when he came over, he was showing signs of affection to my mom, and I was just giving him the cold shoulder. I was furious. I'm not really sure what bothered me the most. I think just seeing him that way, he kind of gave me the creeps, the way he would hold my mom's hand or whatever. I didn't like that he was a friend of my father's. The whole package just turned me off.

That night after he left, my mom was like, "What's the problem here?" And I was like, "I don't like him." And she was like, "But you already know him!" I was like, "I know. But I don't want you seeing him." And she was like, "Okay. If you don't like him, obviously this is not going to work out, because I want to date somebody that you like also." So I was like, "I don't like him." That was it.

It made me feel really good, because she was willing to pick somebody that both of us liked. If she ever did get married again to somebody, she wasn't going to create this stepdaughter-stepfather conflict, which was really nice. And that's why we have this nice set-up that we have now with my stepfather, who is just great.

Some information is necessary for kids to know. Then there is the kind of information that does a child absolutely no good to hear.

Tom, 12 They didn't tell me until a little bit later that they got divorced because of another woman, Colleen. I met the woman, but I didn't know it was the reason for the divorce for a long time, like five years.

My mom just told me one day, right off the bat. "Do you know the reason why the divorce happened?" The divorce seems like it happened a million years ago, so far back, so it was weird to even think about why it happened. "It was because of Colleen." And I was like, "Oh, my God, it was because of Colleen? Colleen?!" I didn't like her to start with. Then I didn't like her even more. My dad's family hated her. The only one who thought even a little bit highly of her was my dad.

Loretta, 21 When I stopped idealizing Dad, I realized he could be irresponsible. I think I thought he would always be responsible. Even when he said he was leaving, I didn't foresee him being irresponsible. But he just did things that outright humiliated us.

For example, my brother's a basketball player. He's in a competitive league, and he's been named one of the best players in the state. It's his big thing, and he loves it. But Dad would come to his games sometimes with his girlfriend and sometimes without. Mom would be there, of course, and Dad would flirt with every woman in the stands. Even married women who are the mothers of Hugh's friends. I mean, he was just terrible.

My brother knew what was going on, and he couldn't hit a single shot, he couldn't pass, he couldn't do anything. It was one thing for my father to be irresponsible out of our sight, but to show up at Hugh's games and act like that. And, of course, it was terrible for my mom, too, sitting there watching him doing this, just wanting to kill him.

He once said to me, "You may find me to be a different person because living with your mother, I've been so unhappy that I haven't been myself." I imagine he said something similar to my brothers. I think he was using that as an excuse, as if he was bringing out his real self or something. I think he was going off the deep end and just freaking out. He kept saying, "Well, you know I never really dated anyone but your mother, and I'm gonna date and have fun now." He was dating this woman who was so much younger and so immature. I don't know what they ever could have had in common on a serious level.

Nicole, 19 One of my friends was dating the son of the guy my mom was dating, and that was always so weird. My mom would go out with him to dinner or something, and they'd go back afterward. She'd be saying good-bye and see my friend pull up, and she'd see her say good-bye to her boyfriend. My mom would say, "I saw your friend over at dinner the other night." And I'd be like, "Oh, gosh, this is strange!"

My dad did the same thing. The son of the woman he was dating, was in one of my classes in junior high. We actually sat at the same art table where the teacher placed us. He'd say things like, "Oh, yeah, your dad came over last night," and I'd think, "I haven't heard from my dad in five days. How come you get to see him all the time?"

Heather, 6 If I had three wishes, I'd want a brother or a sister, I'd want me to have more toys, and I'd want my mother to have a boyfriend. I think she'd be happier that way, like Barbie has Ken.

Barb, 18 I had a big problem with the thought of my mom being involved with a guy. I don't know why. There was this one guy who was helping out a lot in the house, and he would help us with homework, and we'd joke around. But I started getting some inklings that it was a little more than just friendship. They were never demonstrative in front of us or anything, but I got some inklings, and I started to feel uncomfortable. I told my mom, "I don't wanna see him around anymore." My mother listened to me, and he was no longer there. You see, I had a lot of power within the family, a lot of power. I said, "I don't want you marrying. It makes me so uncomfortable." She did not marry, and she didn't see this guy anymore.

Loretta, 21 My mom and her boyfriend are engaged, and I'm the only one who knows it because she hasn't wanted to tell my brothers.

She doesn't want to shake them up because if she marries him, she's not gonna marry him until after my brothers are both in college, at the minimum, and maybe not until after my older brother's out of college.

Christina, 19 I wasn't really uncomfortable with the idea of my mom being with someone, you know, sexually, but I kind of really didn't want to know about it. Like if I heard it going on, I would put headphones on.

Fred, 9 Dad calls his girlfriends "friends" but not baby or honey. Sometimes it's okay, and sometimes it isn't. The way I think it's bad is that he may get obsessed with her, because he hasn't had a person for seven and a half years, and then he may forget about me. I already have a problem with people forgetting about me. I just feel it might be coming. I hope it won't happen, but I think about it.

Cassandra, 19 My mom would spend a lot of time with her fiancé because he was a guy who was also working through some things. So she was over at his place a lot, and I remember feeling a little bit abandoned. I got really upset one day, and I was like, "I feel like you've abandoned me because you're never here, and I have to go and get my own groceries." Stuff like that. It was just a really difficult time.

She feels terrible about it. Sometimes now in joking I'll say, "You abandoned me when I was a sophomore." When I look back now, it was really necessary for their development because of what he was going through at that time. I'm glad that she did what she did. I came out of it okay. I'm not, like, damaged for life or anything. But it was difficult.

Loretta, 21 During the summer when I was in Japan, Mom would write me letters talking about her boyfriend's nine-year-old little girl, how wonderful she was and how she reminded her of me. And I was really hurt because I felt like, "Oh, so this girl's replaced me now?" She was saying, "She likes to read, and you really like to read," and part of that is, I was the only girl, and I was really upset because she would write pages and pages talking about her. Here I am, jealous of a nine-year-old, you know?

I finally called her and told her that I felt she was trying to replace me. Then she said, "It's not like that at all." Later I understood more about their relationship. It isn't this idealized mother-daughter thing, and it isn't like the relationship we have, of course. All these things became obvious later on. In an emotional sense I can see now that it's different.

And as soon as I met her, I could see that it was different. I think Mom was trying to make her letters to me all happy and wonderful and "everything's great," but she exaggerated what it was like. So then I saw that, no, it didn't just instantly become this wonderful relationship or anything like that.

But I am still kind of uncomfortable around her. I don't know why because I'm usually not uncomfortable with kids, but I sort of know she might become my stepsister. I've never had a sister, and I've always wanted an older sister, not a younger one.

Nicole, 19 I saw each of my parents go through a relationship that I thought was going to be the one, where I thought they were going to get remarried, and in each case I absolutely loved the person to death and I loved their kids, and I thought, "My parent would be extremely happy with this person. I wish they would just get on with it and realize that not all marriage is bad." I would have loved to have had them as stepparents and as stepbrothers and -sisters. But both of them ended just because of picky little reasons. Both my parents had problems with their marriage that they've carried with them, and I think they're both scared to get into another marriage. It's always strange when you think something is that set and then, all of a sudden, no. "I can't get past the original relationship, so I can't do this." I haven't had to deal with remarriage or anything, but they've both been serious with people.

Riza, 18 It's funny, I just took these weddings as a fact of life, like, "Okay, we're getting married now." Not that it really changed much of anything. It was just like, "Okay, they're having their little ceremony. This is like when I have a birthday. And then tomorrow it will be over, and they'll open their presents and then go back home."

Twelve

STEPFAMILIES: From Cinderella to the Brady Bunch

Whether remarriage involves one person joining a family, such as a new stepdad, or the blending of two big families full of kids of varying ages from various parents, the members of stepfamilies have many complicated issues to confront. Problems stemming from the divorce that were not adequately resolved at that time have a way of exploding when moms and dads get remarried. Remarriage is a time when parents must talk with their children and listen to what they have to say even if it is not what they want to hear.

Riza, 18 My dad grew up as the son of divorced parents—and divorced grandparents, for that matter. Divorces are all over my family. I have one set of grandparents that haven't gotten divorced. Even my stepdad's parents got divorced and remarried. I used to love going around at the Fourth of July parade saying, "I have eleven grandparents." People would look at me because as a little kid I had this thing that I could do. I would say, "Well, my mom has one set, and then my dad has two sets, and . . ." You know, some grandparents have adopted grandchildren, and some grandchildren have adopted grandparents. It works out that way. When birthdays came around, it was wonderful. Birthdays, holidays, people just came streaming in.

Cassandra, 19 I have a stepdad now. My mom and he got

married when I was a senior in high school, and he is the best father that I could ever ask for. He's just awesome.

They met at church. They dated for about a year, so they started dating when I was a sophomore. And then they got married after that. I thought he was cool right from the start because I've never had a dad in my life, ever. I mean, my mom did remarry to this guy who was just a jerk. And she basically married him because shortly after she got divorced, she felt that she couldn't support herself and me. She did it for security reasons. Then she realized it was just stupid, so they got divorced shortly after. Then for most of my life it's been my mother and me, which has been great. She and I are really close.

But I've always kind of wanted a dad who was real, someone who is always there. And my stepdad is definitely that person. He has a son who's six months older than me and two daughters who are thirteen and eleven now. And that was fun, too, getting some siblings and stuff, because I'm an only child. My stepbrother liked it as much as I did because he has only two little stepbrothers from his mom's remarriage. So he was getting a sister who was his age, and we could hang out. And my stepsisters, when I met them, they were kind of at the age where somebody older than them who was a girl was kind of somebody to look up to. So they look up to me. We do all the little sister things. It was really fun. I think we're all happy to get new siblings. It was a kind of "meant-to-happen" sort of thing. I'm really grateful for that.

Paul, 9 All of a sudden I had two sisters when my dad got married. I was like, "Uh-oh." I never really wanted sisters. Now that I have them, I know why. Only kidding. Mostly. But I like it at Christmas, though. There are a lot more presents now.

What Jewel describes is a perfect example of how not to plan a remarriage.

Jewel, 18 My parents divorced right before I turned thirteen, and my father got remarried on my birthday, two weeks after the divorce.

My mother had this tradition where she would come into our rooms at the exact hour that we were born and sing "Happy Birthday" very quietly, because I was born at two-thirty in the morning, so she never woke me up. My brother, fortunately, was born at six at night. But anyway, she'd come in and she'd sit there through my entire birthday morning. She would wake up, sit there, and experience the whole process of having her children all over again, every year. My birthday was a very, very important day because she worked for ten years to have children with this asshole.

So it was very important for her, and he took me away on that day. That was the first day that she didn't get to come into my room. I could have been at the wedding later on instead of being there the night before. My mom was like, "Can you please just have me drive her up there that afternoon so that I can have my night?" "No."

He wanted us to be there, knowing good and well that we didn't want to be with him. He called the district attorney, said, "Blah blah blah. This is what's going on, and you need to make these children come because it's in our contract." So my mom's lawyer called and said, "Listen, you have to let them go," and we cried the entire way there. We went through the ceremony, and I had to hold the rings for him for this woman that I knew when I was twelve years old when my dad was having an affair with her in Maryland. I had to stand there on my birthday.

It was my thirteenth birthday. In my family we had these landmark birthdays, and thirteen is one of them. "You are a teenager now. You are becoming an adult." I mean, my mom's heart is just very festive and very into these traditions, so this was a very bad one for my dad to disrespect, and that's what he did.

Nick, 17 My parents are still real good friends. They talk, and they're both real active in my life and my sister's life. My stepdad and my stepmom, they're all friends. It's pretty good. I mean, they can be in the same room together and not fight.

Sally, 6 My mom is married to Mohan. I call him Dad. I like him, but I like my dad better because he belongs to me.

Robin, 19 I was rude to Dad's wife, and Dad didn't like it. I didn't like her for the sole reason that he tried to make me like her. If she just had been there, I wouldn't have cared, but he was always like, "Give her a hug good-bye," and I would roll my eyes purposely and be like, "I don't even know her. Get off me." I can't justify it. It was rude. But I'd probably do it again. I guess if it was me, I wouldn't try to force someone. I'm sure she's really nice, but it was just that I never really got a chance to meet her.

It's his fault, 'cause he was all dumb about it. I think he wanted to speed up the process, but he just made it much worse. I remember her being at his house all of a sudden. I was doing a puzzle, and she was there. I think that was the first day that I had met her, but I didn't really talk to her. He had one of those half-and-half heart necklaces. I think he really just tried to make it better because he was like, "Robin, look." Bad move if your kids are already upset. It would make me so mad. I was just like, "That's stupid."

Barb, 18 It's my dad's third marriage now. He's emotionally needy. He needed a wife, is what he always said, and he has actively gone out in pursuit of one.

The second marriage didn't turn out so well. That marriage was really a surprise. Mom and Dad got divorced in March, and he got married in May. He left for China on a trip, he said, and he sent me a postcard. "I'm in China right now. This is going to be an interesting trip," and something like, "When I come back, I'll have something very interesting, a very nice surprise for you," or something like that.

And he came back with a wife. I still have that postcard because I think that was the bluntest way he could have addressed the issue, and it was so jarring that I couldn't throw this postcard away. To tell your kid by postcard in an enigmatic hint that you're getting married, but you had not heard of this woman before . . .

And now the third wife, which happened last year, doesn't speak any English at all, and this one has a son. He speaks English, kind of. I think he's in his second or third year of high school. I'm not sure. He's a pretty shy boy. I don't think he feels as uncomfortable around me as he used to. He used to run into the house, run upstairs, run downstairs if he needed to get something from the kitchen, run downstairs if he needed to do laundry, run back upstairs, close his door, and then he never emerged from the room. Now he feels comfortable watching TV downstairs in front of me a little bit, but he's not completely comfortable. I'm making a big effort with him. Who else is gonna do it? He's too shy to, and I don't want any more tension. And it's ridiculous if I'm the only one speaking English, and Dad is the only translator, you know?

At first I thought he knew no English, so that was really awkward. Just day-to-day things are kind of odd. You kind of do hand signals. The wife knows a couple of words, like "dollars" and "car" and "go" and stuff like that.

There are these horrible movies where some yokels find, like, a bunch of Native Americans and try to speak in their native dialect or something, try to relate to them. They end up sounding like idiots, and it's very offensive overall. Well, that's kind of what I sound like, you know? Trying to piece together words that I think she knows. I guess you kind of learn to live with it. What else are you gonna do? You adapt.

The food is demarcated—his food, my food—and the lines are hazy as to who buys the food in the household. I don't know who to ask. I ask my dad, but he says, "Sometimes I do it, sometimes my wife does it." But how can I speak to his wife, if she's doing grocery shopping, about what I want? He said, "We can put a shopping list on the door." Well, that doesn't really help because she doesn't know English. Sometimes I go out and buy my own stuff, or sometimes I get my mom to do it. It's messy.

Ted, 12 My stepmom was really nice at first, but now she just acts like a mom.

Roberta, 16 Mom was talking to me one day, and she said, "Well, how would you feel if Harry and I got married?" And I was like, "That would be pretty cool." So we wrote him a note, and we left it on his car at work. And he came home that night, and we said, "Will you marry us?" Because it was a package deal. If you're marrying her, you're marrying the whole T-ball team, you're marrying the soccer team, you're marrying the Brownie troupe, you're marrying everything.

Jewel knew that for many years prior to her parents' separation, her father had been having an affair with the woman who eventually became Jewel's stepmother.

Jewel, 18 I have my father's new attached family that he inherited through that woman, and I do have a good relationship with those people. Actually, right now I don't really know if I have a good relationship with them because the last time I talked to my father, all the anger from the past culminated. I went off about how much I despise that woman and how much I couldn't stand to be in the house with her and him. I certainly didn't blame it all on her. It takes two to tango, and my dad is probably at more fault. I will never know exactly how it came about, and I don't really want to know, but I cannot stand to be around her. I'm the kind of person who always makes it known how I feel about somebody. I'm not fake. Out of the love that I still have for my father, I tried to be good, I tried to be caring, and I tried to understand because I've been in relationships, and you can't hate the person for falling out of love with somebody.

I tried to give her the benefit, and finally I just said, "You know, I hate her. She embodies all the pain that you've caused me every time I saw her. It's all reflected on her. And when she tries to step in the business of my family, she will be shot down."

So I told my father this. What I didn't know was that my father had me on speakerphone with her listening, and she then wrote a scathing letter to me. Apparently she has eavesdropped on pretty much every conversation that I've had with my father since they've been together, and so I'm not allowed to see them anymore, and that's fine. But it's the whole idea that they're trying to make me feel bad for saying what I felt.

While Jewel describes a stressful stepfamily situation made even worse by poor judgment on the part of her father, Riza's parents have managed their situation with tolerance and patience.

Riza, 18 At first my stepmom and I had kind of a problem. I wanted to be close to her and she kind of wanted to be close to me, but it just wasn't happening. I mean, we had to force it, and neither one of us wanted to force it. She was upset at some things that I did, and I was upset at some things that she did. We didn't click. Now we're really close. The two of us will sit around and joke about my dad.

My stepdad's another story. It's not so much that we don't get along. It's just that we don't anything. We don't really talk. He's just not the kind of person I can relate to at all. I mean, he's a great dad, but the two of us never really hit it off. So we really stick to basics, like, "Good morning," and saying good-bye when one of us leaves the house, but that's about it. Every once in a while there are awkward spots. When I was living there, if I wanted to ask somebody for the car, I'd always ask my mom, and then she'd have to ask him.

So it wasn't like we'd ever said, "I'm not talking to you. I hate you," or anything. But it's just that we have this real cold sort of nothing between us. Sometimes it gets painful for my mom because she really doesn't like being in the middle of all this. But we all know that nothing's really going to be happening with it anytime soon.

Christina, 19 Oh, yeah, my dad had failed as a father, but he was my father. He loved me, and it's been very hard for me to try to build a relationship with him. I want to have a relationship with him, because you only get one dad. Even if your mom remarries, to a certain extent you only get one dad. And because my mom hasn't remarried, this is very much the case even though I sort of found other dads.

Anne, 9 My stepdad takes me places. We do lots of fun stuff. When I try to describe him, I usually use the word "Dad" because people think it's funny to call him by his name. But I'm not used to that, so I usually just call him by his real name. Whenever I do call him "Dad," my mom says I don't have to. But I think he likes it. It's kind of weird, because if I do call him "Dad," I'm afraid I'll be upsetting my dad, and if I don't, I'm afraid I'll be upsetting him. Sometimes when I'm talking to my real dad about him, I'll call him "Dad," and my real dad gets confused, and I wonder if my real dad is getting mad. So it's confusing. I would like not to feel scared to call them both the same thing, but it's just something that I'm not good at doing.

Roberta, 16 I had to wait until I was eight to get my first Barbie. My little half-sister got hers when she was four. Because there's such an age gap, I see her growing up, and I compare: "You never treated me like that." But then at the same time, things were a lot different. I mean, she has both her parents in the house. There's a lot more under the tree because there are two incomes. I don't feel resentful of them getting what they get. Well, maybe a couple of times. But what am I going to do? Rewind back to when I was four and say, "No! I want a Barbie, Mom"?

Sometimes I wish that she and my little half-brother would realize what they have. They jump around and say, "Oh, Uncle Frank's coming." That's what they call my dad, Uncle Frank. I don't think they realize he's my dad and that Harry is my stepdad. They don't know that I'm not their whole sister because they don't understand that. But the real thing they understand is that I'm their big sister. Harry had a son from before, and they don't really get that he's my stepbrother but he's their half-brother. We don't do the whole "step" and "half" thing. They'll understand later that Harry's not my real dad, that Uncle Frank is my dad, but it doesn't occur to them what it's like not to have their dad living in the house. So I don't resent them because of it. They're four and five. How can I say, "Appreciate this!" I can't.

So, sometimes it's weird when I hear them screaming and going on, complaining that they didn't get a toy at McDonald's or Grandma bought them this but didn't buy them that. And I want to say, "You got a toy! You got to go to McDonald's. We went out once a month, and McDonald's was the biggest deal in the world." I can't even tell you what a big deal going to McDonald's was when I was their age, and they're saying, "McDonald's, whatever." So sometimes I look at them and say, "You guys are so spoiled."

Even sometimes Mom is like, "Roberta, you need to back off them because they don't know any better. Sorry I couldn't get you a Barbie. Sorry I couldn't do better." I'll be playing out stuff like, "Oh, look at this. I didn't get this." Mom'll say, "Roberta!" And then I'll feel guilty and back off.

Barb, 18 Dad and his second wife were together for eight years, and it just didn't work out. She became very unhappy. She was not comfortable with my brother and me. My dad explained it later on that she was, like, astrologically wrong for him, something like that. He went and got his love charts or something examined by some Chinese guy and found that, yes, my mother was wrong for him and, yes, he should have checked the love charts before marrying these women.

That's complete bullshit because he must have consulted these same kinds of love charts for this current wife, who's not really working out that well, either. But he said he's going to stick with it because he doesn't want any more divorces. And she is a very devoted Christian. Since he married her, my dad has become a born-again Christian.

Tom, 12 With both of my stepparents, it's kind of implanted in my brain that "okay, this is the new routine. It's going to be for many years." I don't think they'll get divorced. I shouldn't say this because with my mom and my dad, it wasn't gonna last forever. But there is this certainty about my stepparents that they just belong together for the rest of their lives.

Riza, 18 My dad's first remarriage, I remember them living together, being very comfortably open around the house. A very affectionate couple. Same thing with my dad and his current wife. I mean, they were building something. They had both been hurt really badly in previously relationships, so they were establishing all these new parameters for the new household. For a really long time —and even now—they go into the "making the rules" kind of thing. There's a rule that the kids get out of the living room at nine o'clock at night because that's the Mom and Dad time. They get to sit and watch their soap operas or whatever they watch. Then as their kid hit adolescence, it wasn't fair because she wanted to watch those shows, too. So now she has a TV in her room, and she has no excuse when it comes to getting out of the living room.

When I was getting near eighteen, I would go there for visits over the summer, and it got to be "Can Riza stay in the living room because Riza's like an adult now?" But my sister's five years younger than me, and she got really bitter. She's like, "No, there's no way she can stay in the living room and I can't." I wanted to avoid conflict, so I said, "Never mind. I just won't." So then they got her that TV for her room and solved the problem.

But there are all these rules. There's the whole thing of how many meals a week we're all going to have together. It started out very structured. Now we're slowly breaking down the structure because it's becoming more of a burden. But before, the structure was necessary to build the family. At first we had, like, a three-course dinner every night that my stepmom would cook. It was a great family bonding sort of experience, but after a while she was like, "I can't cook this much anymore."

All these things took considered decisions, especially the way my father is. My father is less and less like this, but he used to ramble on forever. I mean, he'd start talking, and there'd be no end. And then he'd start going off on these tangents and talking about all this other stuff. We'd sit around on a Saturday, and they'd lay out the new ground rule. And they'd explain the background and why we're doing this and that, and three, four, five hours later, my sister and I would be like, "Okay, so we're not going to have family dinner tonight?"

There was a lot of that, the family structure kind of stuff, both before they got married and after. And constantly ever since. But we're letting go of more stuff now, just sort of throwing it to the wind, because at this point we are more of a family.

Fred, 9 When she married somebody else, at first it was uncomfortable. It was like a shock. At first when you meet somebody new, it is weird when he's becoming part of your family. I had bad dreams about him. I dreamed he started beating my head like a drum with drumsticks. Then he took a human head and started playing the hair like guitar strings. It was scary, a real nightmare.

Jessica, 16 I'd had my mom to myself over the last couple of years, and he comes to me and it's "There's no more Road Runner cartoons Saturday morning, with everyone hopping into bed." So there was no more nap. There were no more reading nights at the table. We all love to read. Mom and my brother and I really get into it. We would just sit around the dinner table and read, and maybe talk a little.

We had a thing called Munch a Bunch where we would just go into the kitchen and make whatever you wanted for dinner, but you had to have the four food groups represented. So you would get an apple and put peanut butter and raisins on it, and then you'd make a peanut butter sandwich with something on it. And you'd sit at the table with that. And my stepdad's not really into that. He likes to have a cooked meal and sitting around the table talking, conversing, praying, even. Not like we all sit around and pray. We hold hands and pray.

Anyway, it was like little things that changed, but they were still important. But they were important things that I was willing to give up because Mom was happy. She was not happy before my stepdad. You could tell. She was tired all the time. She would cook wrong. She would be depressed. She would try to be cool around us, like, "All is bright." But you could tell that she wasn't cool. And she seemed happy when they first got married. Definitely.

And it got her off our backs. As much as I want to say we had this perfect thing, she was in our faces. She knew everything that was going on. If we forgot our keys one day and hopped through the window, she knew. So with him around, it was sort of a little distraction.

Jewel, 18 I remember the first night that my dad and his wife were together. They were in this apartment that he had taken while he was still trying to decide whether he was going to move away or stay in town and have that plan thing that they give every divorced family, for the child to go back and forth on the weekends.

On that first weekend I was crying on the way, and I was yelling, "I can't stand to be around you. I hate you, I hate you, I hate you," and she butts in. She's Korean and doesn't speak very good English, and she smacks me and says, "You disrespect your father!" And I'm just like, "Oh!" I just couldn't handle it.

So I just yelled and yelled and yelled, and my poor little brother, who was very nonconfrontational, was sitting over in the corner, eyes popping out of his head. He was just like, "I am so scared." I was always the voice, because my brother never could stand up to our father. So I have always been my brother's voice. I just had to be much louder and obnoxious than any thirteen-year-old needs to be. I knew too much about life.

Anne, 9 I went to the father-daughter dance with my stepdad, which was great because he's a good dancer!

Riza, 18 After a while I kind of got used to my stepmom. Just from the start they were the cutest couple. Her daughter, who was then six, in that first year she kind of had an attitude, an edge with my dad. It's not that she didn't like him. It was just because she had had a bad experience with her mother's previous boyfriend who was not too great. He'd lock her in her room. Her own father was never around because as soon as her mom got pregnant, he disappeared. So all told, she never really had a father, and her mother's boyfriend was a bad guy.

So she had a problem for a while adjusting to my dad. A few years later they went through a whole process of adoption. Now they're really close, and she's actually my half-sister. It's kind of nice. Immediately, they became this tight-knit family. They got married when I was twelve. I mean, it's nice because I don't have a sibling rivalry thing. She's so much younger that she looks up to me. She's like, "Wow, you're so cool." I'm like her second mom. I'll be sitting in my room doing my homework, and she'll come in and say, "Can I just sit in here and draw?" It's like "Riza's room, the shrine."

Cassandra, 19 I've met my half-brothers a couple of times, and I know one of them is married down in Arkansas and just had a little girl. In fact, my dad, in my birthday card, sent me a picture of my half-brother with my new niece. And he said something like, "This is Ferell with his daughter." It's the first I heard of her, and I'm like, "Great, what am I supposed to do? She's seven months old already." So I have no relationship with them.

Actually, I tried to have a relationship with one of them who I kind of hung out with a little bit when my dad was here. The three of us went out several years back, and I sent him a birthday card. I never received any sort of communication back, so I thought, "Okay, I guess you just don't want to be my brother."

I don't really care. They're much older. One is twenty-eight, and the other is twenty-six.

I pretty much always knew they existed. There was never a day when all of a sudden my mother was like, "Oh, did you know you have half-brothers?" and my life changed. I actually learned of it when I was real young, and my dad was visiting one time. My mom said something like, "He's staying with your half-brothers." "Oh, okay. Where did they come from?"

Roberta, 16 I felt really bad. I didn't know what to call my stepdad because I see my real dad only once or twice a year. I didn't want to call Harry "Dad" because I felt like, "I don't want to erase my dad's memory," even though I don't really see him that much. But it just felt weird calling Harry "Dad." When Mom was growing up, her mom and dad adopted two boys, and the two boys called her dad "Sarge" because he was in the military. They didn't want to call him "Mister So-and-So" or just by his first name, and they decided on "Sarge."

So we tried a few things like that, but it seemed really fake and I just didn't like it. So I pretty much just call him Harry. Recently I asked him to the daddy-daughter dance at my school, and he told me on the way home about how it was really hard at first. But we have a really good relationship now because we had to start out being friends first.

And it's really cool because he's really one of the greatest guys I know. We had to become friends before I could be his daughter and he could be my dad. We've gotten to that point where I call him "Dad" sometimes, or I do a lot more things with him than I do with my real dad. So it's like he is my dad. But I usually call him Harry because he's more of my friend. Now it would be too weird to call him "Dad." Not because of the whole erasing-Dad's-memory thing. It has nothing to do with that. It would just be weird after all this time.

Robin, 19 I only remember meeting her once, and then he said, "I'm getting married. Do you wanna come?" And I started laughing, and then he got mad and I never went. I was a mean child. But I'd never met her, and I wasn't happy with it to start with. I didn't even really get along with him anymore, and all of a sudden it's like, "Hey, you wanna come?" I was just like, "No."

I know that my older sister went. I don't know if my brothers did or not.

Tom, 12 I've gotten used to seeing my stepparents kiss. When my mom got married, it was awkward, and when Lane and my dad got married, it wasn't because I was already through the first one. So it was easy the second time around.

Jamal, 20 I have a half-brother. I didn't really pay attention to the "half" part because when you live with somebody, he is just a big brother. My brother's eight years older than me. My sister's four years older. She's also my half-sister, but we were all just one unit.

Roberta, 16 In 1990, Mom got pregnant, so Harry quit smoking. We had a porch and we had ashtrays out there. It wasn't a big deal because Harry never smoked in the house. We said from the beginning, "No smoking in the house. That's disgusting."

Then he said, "Well, you're pregnant, so I'll quit completely." That was definitely the roughest time, him quitting smoking. It's just a normal nicotine withdrawal thing, but they had just gotten married. It was like, "What the hell? This guy just comes in and starts yelling at us? God, she married an ass!"

Riza, 18 Whether my dad wanted to or not, he sort of learned the yelling thing from his dad. When he got angry, he'd yell. So since his recent marriage, his new wife made it very clear to him that she will not tolerate any yelling. She's really cool about it. She'll just say what she won't have, and that's the way it's going to be. At first I held a little bit of that against her. "She's got my dad wrapped around her little finger, and how come she can make all these rules and stuff?" I was getting kind of defensive, like, "Who is this woman to come and take over my dad? He can yell if he wants to."

But now I really appreciate it because ever since he got her, he's been working so hard to tone himself down. Now it takes a lot to get him to yell. If the two of them have a problem, often they end up talking about it. But ever since they met, they've never had a yelling, screaming fight. I remember my thirteen-year-old sister—when we were both a little younger and the children would be in their room, and the door was shut and you could hear that they were talking—she'd come and ask, "Are Mommy and Daddy having a fight?" And I'd say, "No, they're just discussing." So it's been this really peaceful sort of constructive relationship. I really admire that.

Roberta, 16 Mom arranged this so well. I had a friend whose dad was quite wealthy. So we used to go and stay at their houseboat on the weekends. Mom met Harry, and she invited him over to the house for dinner on one of the weekends that we weren't going to be at home.

By this time the three of us, my mom, brother, and I, we were really close. We could tell each other's moods so fast. And for so long we'd been Mom's sole support system, so we could tell when she was in a good mood. This time she was in a really good mood when we got back, and we're like, "Hey, what's up?" We knew something happened, and she was like, "I met someone!" But we had hated all her other boyfriends. They were so gross.

Tom, 12 It's been so long that I don't even regard it as "my parents used to be married." I actually don't even remember much because it's been so long, and it's been implanted in my brain that they've been separated for so long. They were only together for, like, two years and six months out of my whole entire life of twelve years.

Now I have a baby half-sister. It's fun. She's so cute. But I don't change her diaper.

Fred, 9 Having a stepfather makes me feel special. I don't have a stepmother.

When I first met my stepfather, I thought, "This is like shit." It was like, "I don't know you. This is weird. You look funky," because he had long hair when I first met him. I thought, "Is this guy a fashion nightmare or what?"

Roberta, 16 He had to live with us first for six months. We don't go into the whole Catholic thing anymore. So she said to him, "I'm going to date you, then you have to live with us. You have to see exactly what's going on. You have to see that it's not this great, perfect people thing. Like on Saturday morning, you have to get up at the crack of dawn to go to soccer practice. In the middle of the night, someone will puke all over you in the bed."

It was cool. We went to his place, and it was such a pigsty. He gets mad about that and says, "It wasn't a pigsty!" But it was him and his roommate living there, so of course it was a mess. But we got his stuff and brought it in. He brought a waterbed, which we thought was great. To me it was just like, "Yeah, cool. Now you're here." My mom's mom had lived with us a couple of different times, and her one sister and her brother, too. We'd had people moving in and out all the time, of all types. And so having a new person come in and stay didn't really affect me. And being married down the road wasn't going to change things once he moved in. It would be the same.

Riza, 18 I was an only child for twelve years, and then within two years I got three siblings.

Nick, 17 To tell you the truth, since I moved out from my mom's and came here to my dad's, I miss my friends more than my family. I just didn't get along there. I mean, I had a couple of fights with my stepdad. He used to drink a lot, and he used to get so stupid and make like the biggest deal out of nothing, so we got into some shoving matches. There was one time I just left the house and spent the night with my friend Pete.

Barb, 18 My best friend says, "Why don't you just go back to your mom's house. It seems a lot easier than all that stuff with your stepfamily." But no, it's not. It's so much more stressful at my mom's. At least at my father's house there are long spans of time when no one's in the house, and that's what I treasure the most. The house doesn't have too much furniture in it because he and his wife and my stepbrother just recently moved into it. I feel comfortable when I'm the only one in the house and I'm alone.

Roberta, 16 It never occurred to me that they're any different because they are my little "half-sister" and little "half-brother." Mom asks that all the time, but it doesn't even cross my mind. It's never "You're not my real brother and sister. I don't have to take care of you." I can't scream it loud enough: "It doesn't even cross my mind." Never occurs to me.

Thirteen

PARENTS, CHILDREN, AND DIVORCE: You've Changed! No, You've Changed!

Divorce can improve some parent-child relationships. It is not unusual to find, for example, that a workaholic parent spends more time with a child after a divorce when a schedule has been arranged and the time seems so much more precious.

There is also the flip side, where problems between parent and child that have been smoldering are brought to a full blaze in the midst of divorce.

Wayne, 17 I feel more comfortable around my dad because I can talk to him, not just because he's my father. I can talk to him like he's my best friend. We get along perfectly. My mom, she treats me like I'm still a little kid, you know?

Christina, 19 Dad came out for my eighteenth birthday. I don't think that it occurred to him that, turning eighteen, there were places I'd rather be than with my dad, but there we were.

Cassandra, 19 My dad told me to call him whenever I needed money, like to help me pay bills and my rent and stuff like that, no questions asked. And I was running out of money the last quarter last year. I needed rent money really bad, so I called him, and all hell broke loose. He was like, "I can't give you that much money. I can maybe give you a hundred dollars. Why do you always call me whenever you need money?''

And that statement is really a reflection on his two sons, my half-brothers, who do call him only for money, whereas I was calling to talk to him, to tell him what's going on in my life. And sometimes I would need money.

A lot of times I've felt, when I was having a relationship with him, that I was using him, because I don't know my dad. I can honestly tell you I don't know him at all. I always felt our relationship was really shallow, like there wasn't much there. I was also thinking, "I call you to talk to you, and you never call me. How can we have anything more than this shallow relationship if you never call me?" His excuse is that he doesn't want to talk to that other man at the house, my stepdad; he says he's afraid or he just doesn't want to deal with him or blah blah blah. I mean, please! That just doesn't make sense. I'm his daughter. I'm the same blood he is. He shouldn't not call me just because my stepdad is there. So when he said that I only call him for money, well, this is a two-way street, buddy.

Roberta, 16 We get along, but I think I remind him too much of Mom. Not in a bad way, but there are things I say or gestures or even my personality. I don't think it pisses him off or anything. If it does, at least he makes it so I can't tell.

Both Cassandra and Jewel have already experienced the loss of their relationships with their fathers. Their hope at this point is that some sort of resolution in these relationships can happen before their losses becomes absolute.

Cassandra, 19 He's old. He has heart problems. He'll probably die, and I will have to say that I never really knew him, which is kind of sad. Maybe he'll die when we're not speaking, and then I'll probably have this big guilt thing going on. I'd like to be on good terms with him before he dies, but it's just real difficult for me. I'd feel like I was doing it because I didn't want to feel so guilty when he passed away. I would feel like I wasn't really seriously investing in the relationship.

Jewel, 18 He has this idea in his head that he is an infallible, omniscient jerkoff. He does not feel that anything he's ever done is wrong, and he doesn't feel that he needs to be forgiven for anything. A few years down the road I might say to myself, "Who is my dad?" And he'll be dead and I'll never be able to know.

And my dad is just as much a part of me as my mother—in the biochemical makeup. But my ideas and my personality and pretty much everything else about me is my mother.

Nicole, 19 He and I are a lot alike in the things that we find amusing. We both love to play jokes on people and to do fun things. We both love to be out doing things, not just sitting in and watching TV. And I think he's changed a lot in that way since the divorce. Before the divorce he was always like, "I'll just sit here and watch the football game," whereas I think he's a lot more "out" now. He's more willing to actually go out and not just see himself as the father. We have that in common. With my mom, we see the world the same way and react to the world in the same way, but my dad and I have fun in the same ways. I think that makes it all the better that I lived with my mom, but when I go out to do things with my dad, we have great times.

In the beginning that made it difficult on my mom. She would say things like "You see your dad as the fun parent because he takes you out to do fun things and spends money on you and goes to cool places, whereas I'm the disciplinarian, the parent who says, 'Did you do your homework?'" I think she realizes now that we don't see it that way, that we say Mom's the one we'd go to if we have a problem. Dad's the one who, if we have a funny new joke or if we feel like going to see a cool new movie or going boating, we'd talk to him.

So I think she sees that we have a deeper relationship with her. And I think my dad sees that now, too, and it makes it difficult for him. He hates it that he hasn't been as much a part of my life and doesn't know my friends as well as my mom does and doesn't know about all the stupid little assignments I have for school—things like that. But it's not just that we see him as the fun parent and we see her as the strict parent, because that's not the only way it is, either.

Carie provides an example of how a parent-child relationship can improve because of divorce.

Carie, 15 My dad worked a lot. I never saw him much. And then even when he was home, he spent a lot of time cleaning stuff and fixing stuff. When we did do things together, we went to movies and other stuff that didn't require a lot of talking. I don't think anyone was really close to my dad. I think we're actually closer now because he calls every night on the phone. And he comes over fairly often, too. Now he seems to make the time more than before.

Marshall, 17 I'm trying to have a relationship with Mom. When I was a young child, I always thought that she was a really cool mom. My dad was never like, "You know, your mom's a bitch." He never did any of that stupid stuff, so I was able to figure out for myself that Mom was kind of nutso.

Jamal, 20 My father was mean, he was cheap, but he was the most excellent provider I've ever seen. He cared more for us, I think, than he did for himself. He was a good man. My mom was strong and loved us more than the world. I had two good parents. It just came to the point where they weren't together anymore.

My father loved me, but he didn't know how to show it—and still doesn't know how to show it. He does in certain ways—like all my life he never gave me a dollar unless I worked for it, to try to teach me how to work. Every place I go and work, they say, "Man, you've got the best work ethic I've ever seen in my life. Where did you learn how to work like this?" He's the reason I know how to work.

Even now he'll say, "I'm not giving you money. You have to work for it." I mean, he works so hard. He works fifteen hours a day. But my mom—a mother's gonna be a mother. She's gonna love you no matter what you do, no matter what kind of trouble you're in. You can always depend on your mom. At least mine I know I can, no matter what goes on. They were nice together, but they had to split up.

Jewel, 18 Fortunately my grandfather, my mother's father, who died four years ago, turned into my father. That sounds horrible when you say it, but my grandfather was as close as anyone came to being my father. When I lost him, that was so much harder than if I lost my real father. He did everything for me.

Martin, 18 When I was younger and there were father and son things, my father would go. But whenever it wasn't required, he wouldn't. I think there was one time where he did, and that was kind of cool. I appreciated it. It felt special, like, "All right, my dad actually went. We're having fun."

A couple of the other guys' dads would always go, and they became my surrogate fathers. I owe them a lot. I still talk to them quite often. The guy's dad who was a scoutmaster when I was there was very influential in getting me to go to the prom because I hadn't gone to any dances until the prom. He was just like, "You're going whether you want to or not." So I called up a girl I'd been flirting with and asked her, and now we're going out, so I owe him that.

Cassandra, 19 My father and I haven't really gotten along because I've always been two steps ahead of the game. I've always been a little bit more mature for my age. When I first started figuring out that he was kind of immature, I was in middle school. I would say, "Dad, what you're saying, what you're doing, it just does not make any sense."

And it was like talking to a wall. I would say that that's the reason we don't have a relationship. Because I can't look up to him. I can't look up to somebody who doesn't have any sense. I can't respect that person. If he were eight years old, fine. But he's not. He's sixty-something, and I can't take anything he says too seriously because he's just so whacked out.

Christina, 19 I wish he would care. I think he wants to care, but I don't think that makes him care. He wants to feel like he has a relationship with somebody because his second wife left him, his dad's dead, his girlfriends keep leaving him. He has nobody in the world. Biologically, he has my sister and me, so he wants to have something with us. And biologically, I suppose I have him.

Kurt, 16 I'm never going to be "Oh, I love my mom." It's never gonna happen. But I've gotten to the point where I just feel sorry for her. I have to laugh because if someone acts like she does, acts so terrible and has such a rotten heart or maybe no heart at all, down the road you start to pay a terrible price for breaking your family apart and for hurting your children and hurting your husband. The pain that I experience right now or that my father experienced will be so minimal compared to what will happen to her that I feel sorry for her. When that happens to her, she won't have anybody to go to because I won't be there.

Martin, 18 My dad and I had never really talked or did much when I was living with him. It's still the same way now. My mom, she's the original soccer mom. She was a soccer mom before there were soccer moms. She was always there, while my dad was always working. I think it was his big problem. He worked too much. And, yeah, there's that whole deal of "Oh, we need money for security" and all of that.

But what's the point of having money if you can't have fun with it? It doesn't make sense to me to save for your entire life, because by the time you're old enough to enjoy the money, what the hell are you gonna do? You're in a wheelchair in an old people's home.

Nicole, 19 My dad still lives fifteen minutes away from where my mom lives, so I see him all the time. And now that I'm away at school, I talk to him just as much as I talk to my mom, and he and I have actually gotten a lot closer. I think I've started to understand some things that have happened because of the divorce and because of other things that have happened in his life, like fighting in the war and other things he's gone through. I've seen how those things have affected who he is, and it explains some of the things that he does that bother me and the way that he thinks about things. I think I've gotten to be more understanding about that, and at the same time I think he's started to realize that I'm growing up and I'm not his little girl that he has to protect and watch over all the time.

Roberta, 16 Do I feel close to my dad? Not at all. When I'm down there, when I'm visiting with him, we get close. But then I get home, and it's like, "What happened?" We don't talk to each other for, like, two weeks. We don't write to each other. I guess it's kind of cool to pick up wherever we left off, but it's also kind of a "what the hell?" thing, you know? I just got off the phone with him, talking about what I should pack and what he has and what I have, because I'll be leaving soon to go down to him. It's great every once in a while.

Paula, 17 My mom is just very controlling. She's very opinionated, very stubborn. I argued with her ad infinitum, saying, "Do you know anything about me, Mom? Do you know who your daughter is? Do you know what I'm studying? Do you know what I'm interested in? Do you know any of this?" She's like, "No, because you wouldn't come to visit me." Nothing can ever be her fault. And she will never feel sorry for what happened, and the animosity, of course, remains.

Cassandra, 19 I'm kind of happy not associating with my father right now because it's just one of those relationships that's not healthy. You feel when you have it that a weight is coming down, and you feel more free when you don't have it. But I also feel like I have to have it, too. I imagine the door will be opened again, probably sometime in the future. And I hope it's opened by him. I don't want to open it again. It's always been me.

It's funny, because he doesn't know anything. So much has changed in this last year. I'll probably open the door, at least when I get married or something. But then I don't want him walking me down the aisle. I want my stepdad to walk me down the aisle. So then that would be a whole huge problem there, too. I mean, what do you do with that if my dad's alive? If he's not alive, I don't have to worry about it, obviously. I hope the door's open before he dies, but I don't know how much of a relationship I really want to have with the guy.

If he does die, I don't know if I will be contacted. He has no family out there. He's just out there because he likes the weather. He has these fly-by-night friends. When he does die, am I gonna know before he's buried? How am I ever going to find out? Does he have a list of people to call if he dies? I doubt it. I don't think he would be that responsible. Maybe someone would call us, but I just don't know.

Fourteen

MONEY: The Tip of the Iceberg

Money is almost as powerful as a symbol as it is as currency. It can be used to show love. It can be a tool of power, withheld to inflict punishment or dispensed to confer praise. Unfortunately, it is sometimes seen as payment for spending time with one's children, such as when a previously disengaged father demands visitation only after a court petition has been filed for an increase in child support payments to the mother, or when a mother attempts to halt visitation because of a father's failure to pay child support. Money is often used to make up for deficits in a relationship.

Though children may be acutely aware of their family's financial circumstances, what parents do with money is the business of the parents. It is unfair and unnecessary to involve children in the grown-up world of financial problems or in the battles waged over money.

Jamal, 20 Dad had stopped child support payments, and my mom kept me from seeing him, I guess. That's the time when you're trying to fit in at school—not to be popular, just not to be laughed at. You want to just blend in with the crowd.

I couldn't do that. We didn't have enough money. It was just me and my mom. My sister and my brother were away at school, my father wasn't around, and I couldn't fit in without money. I didn't have enough pants to wear a different pair every day of the week, so I had to wear the same pair of pants three days a week. I didn't have nice clothes, which is kind of embarrassing in junior high. Everything has to be name brand, and I just didn't have it. I stood out because I was bigger, so everybody noticed me right away. I honestly thought my mom was taking the money and spending it on whatever.

To this very day my father has to pay child support for college expenses, and he's so mad at my mom that he switched to where he doesn't pay her the child support, he pays directly to me.

Ted, 12 My mom and dad fought over their car. It ended up costing them more to fight over it than it cost to buy a new car. That was pretty stupid.

Loretta, 21 One thing I am terrified about in regard to my dad to this day—and he uses this over my mom as well—is money. He's paying for the student-parent loan for school, and at one point he threatened not to pay it, which would leave me in trouble when I graduate because I have federal loans as well. It would be a sum of money that I couldn't pay back on a monthly basis. It just would not be feasible for me.

So on one level I don't want to make him angry, and my mom's afraid of him in that sense, too, because she knows that if he chooses not to pay child support or not to pay alimony, then the only option is to try to take him back to court. But she can't afford to do that, and how is she gonna track him down? I mean, he really could just renege on the agreement and run off somewhere, and there isn't much we could do.

He uses that power when he feels like he needs to. My mom said something to him recently because I was really freaked out and worried about it. I've been trying to think, "Okay, how can I pay this if, when I graduate, he stops paying?"

I'm going to be real careful and not do this to my kids. I want to go to law school, and as far into debt as I'm going, I don't know if I'll be able to. I feel like they didn't put any savings away for my college, and they should have—from the moment I was born. That's what I'm gonna do for my kids so there will be a fund for them.

Douglas, 13 One thing I can say for my dad is that he gives me plenty of money. I might see him only twice a year, and maybe he won't call at all, but every month or so he sends me cash. He says that it's just a little something extra for me. It's like a hundred bucks each time, and sometimes more.

It pisses my mom off. She tells my aunt that he's just a lowlife trying to buy my love. She's also afraid that I'll buy drugs with the money, which is so stupid. So she wants to take the money and hold on to it for me, for the future. But I get to it first because I get home first every day. So I spend it however I want. But really I save most of it because Mom says my dad won't live forever. She's glad when she says it, but I'm not.

Loren, 15 He didn't call us or talk to us, visit us, write, or nothing. So I had a big chip on my shoulder about this. My mom went to the best lawyer she could find in Seattle. She'd spoken to a lot of women who said, "You have to play hardball because no matter how much you loved a person in a marriage, in divorce they can become a really terrible person, and you have to believe that you deserve what you deserve." Many people feel so good about divorcing that they let the other person take everything.

He had fought a custody fight to keep us and lost. After he left, my mom had to work as a union carpenter because there was not much money to be made as a woman at that time. She had learned how, starting at the bottom. She was a seamstress by profession, and she had also cleaned houses for a living, mowed lawns, and stuff. She always ran her own business. She'd worked for other people, but she was always hustling—and she's hustling still. She now has an antique business as well as her sewing business and a few other things, like she is a doll collector. I respect her a lot. She made it without child support. The state of Washington tried to help her, but at the time there wasn't a really well-established system for catching deadbeat dads. They've improved that since then, and I really applaud that legislature.

Fifteen

MY OWN RELATIONSHIPS: Will I Marry and Have Kids?

While most children I have spoken with have hopes of getting married, many of them harbor serious concerns about how the divorce has affected their capacity, if not their desire, to form and maintain a marriage or marriage-like relationship. Trusting others can be difficult for children who were exposed to highly volatile marriages or divorces, and who themselves had their trust shattered by disappointment and trauma. Many children grow up to view marriage as a forum that allows adults to exert control over others.

As we saw in the chapter on stepfamilies, a good second marriage can actually provide a revised blueprint for future relationships for children. Also, a marriage that is terminated with the parents' dignity intact, and with a commitment to peacefully coparent the children, can help a child learn that mistakes can be fixed. Under these conditions, the idea of marriage can be preserved as something positive instead of something to fear.

Christina, 19 When the example that you have in front of you is divorce, it's so scary to say, "This is the right person that I want to spend the rest of my life with."

Roberta, 16 My theory is, you ever heard of a girls' sleep-over? There's like ten girls, and it always ends up that, say, four go one way, three go into a different room, and there are three that are neutral or one's left out or one's in the middle, and everyone always goes home crying. There's always this big crazy thing. Everyone's gonna go the entire night ignoring each other or fighting or squabbling, or getting along and watching the others fight.

But everyone always ends up thinking they get along, after they fight, then get along, then fight, and the whole thing is this roller coaster from hell. And it seems like marriage is one really long sleep-over. And I hate sleep-overs. They get on my nerves. It's not so easy to stick around. You just wanna be like, "God, you're getting on my nerves. Go away."

Nicole, 19 I often wonder, "Well, gosh, will I ever find somebody that I can actually stick with? Will I ever be able to really commit to somebody? Will I ever be able to get married?"

Everything was so ugly in the end for my parents. They had been so sure that they were in love. They got married, and everything was so fine at the beginning. And then they went through a lot because of the divorce. What's to say that that wouldn't happen to me—where it seems so perfect, but then it wasn't? I'm just scared. I'm afraid the same thing will happen. And not just with marriage but relationships in general, with anything that gets serious.

Amber, 7 When I grow up, I'll just have lots of boyfriends, like Mom. I'll never get married because getting divorced takes too long.

Suzy, 16 I don't really get close to any guys in my life. I don't have a boyfriend or anything because I look at a guy and think, "Ooh! I know what he's gonna do." I'm so caught up in his faults. I don't know if that is because of my parents getting divorced or because my mom's the

161

most raging feminist you'll ever meet in your life. Maybe I've inherited that from her, but I do not trust men.

Guys my age I don't like. They're stupid, they're immature. The guys that I want are in college, and unfortunately that's illegal. I'm just at the wrong age or something. I'm sure it has a lot to do with my parents getting divorced, but I don't know. I don't know if I trust guys enough to fall in love. Maybe that'll happen to me, but as of right now, I don't know.

Heather, 6 I don't know if I'll ever get married. He'd have to be a good man. He'd have to stay at home with us. He could never move away. That's why I don't think I'll ever get married because he would probably have to move away.

Cassandra, 19 I can't really see myself not being married. But it's not something that's on the top of my priority list like it is for a lot of people. I really want to get my whole life together, my career and everything, before I decide to get married. But I think I'll definitely get married.

I am already very, very choosy in who I date. Relationships are a little bit of a problem because usually I just find something that I know just drives me crazy. And then I'll be like, "Oh, I can't deal with you. Good-bye." I don't know if that's because of what I've seen with my mom or if it's just because I'm just really picky and I can't deal with little flaws or whatever. I don't want to make the same mistakes she did. I will not get divorced—I absolutely refuse to—so that means I have to pick the right person from the start. Because divorce is just a pain. It just makes a lot of things more difficult than they should be.

Roberta, 16 It's probably not gonna happen. My expectations are probably way too high. I mean, I'm setting myself up for being the oldest spinster in the world.

Christina, 19 I am going to try not to make the same mistake that I watched other people make. I'm trying to learn different things. That's why I ask everybody about divorce. I try to ask happy couples, and there are a lot of books out on it.

Nicole, 19 The more relationships I see outside of my parents' and the older I get, the more I see that that was not the way it has to be, that that was a really tense, strained relationship.

Shanon, 10 I know I'm only ten, but I know I'll never get married. Mom and Dad say that I will, but I can't wait until I'm old and they see that I didn't. I'll live with friends but never get married.

Sally, 6 I think I'll have at least one kid when I get married. But I really don't want me to die. My mom said the divorce is going to be the death of her. I'm worrying about dying. You should worry about it. It scares me because I don't want it to happen. I don't want my dad to die, too.

Shari, 15 I don't know how I trust people. People say the first relationship you have is with your mom or your dad, and the first person that a girl gets married to is her dad, from what I've heard, and the first person that a boy marries is his mom. I don't wanna marry my dad. I don't wanna marry someone who's going to not be around or is going to divorce me or is gonna be a liar. I don't wanna do that, and I'm not going to settle for that. I don't wanna be grabbing the kids and the furniture and everything, and have to worry about some stupid guy.

Like Barb and Shari, many children have grandparents who can serve as alternative role models for relationships. Grandparents and other trusted adult family members can also offer insights that the child might otherwise have had a hard time seeing.

Barb, 18 I haven't told my mother yet that I'm not ever getting married or having kids. She'd totally freak out. I told my aunt when I went to New York this Christmas, and my aunt is my mother's older sister. She's almost like a grandma to me. I told her that I was never gonna have children and that I was never gonna get married, and she said to me, "Your parents are very selfish people. They cannot think of anyone but themselves. They love you very much, but you can't let them affect the course of your life."

And I know that. Their love for me I've never doubted. However, she said, "You have to separate yourself from them, and you have to know where they went wrong, that they are wrong. When you graduate from college, get away from them as soon as you can. Separate yourself from them emotionally, physically if you have to."

And she was telling me this about her own sister. But it never struck me as an option, as a thing to do. I mean, I can't do that. I can't just switch off a valve and suddenly go numb. How many years have I been like this? I guess it doesn't matter now, trying to understand where I am, who I am. It's really difficult.

Riza, 18 Anytime I told my grandmother about my relationships or anything that was going on in my life, she'd kind of analyze it. When I was having dating problems, she'd always say, "This is an effect of the divorce." I kind of didn't want to hear it. I was like, "Yeah, right." If I went after a guy that I clearly had no chance of getting because he was either already dating somebody else or just one of those unreachable goals, then she'd say that.

And other people do this, too, whether or not they're from divorced families. They say that I'm setting a goal I can't reach because I know I won't reach it. I'm just setting myself up so I won't get hurt, basically. My grandmother said it was a way of protecting myself that I learned through this whole divorce thing. I wonder how right she is. Sometimes I think she might be very right.

So I sometimes try to step outside myself. I do that a lot, try to be introspective, constantly analyzing what I'm doing. I think the combination of the way I am and those experiences makes me double-check things more often just to make sure that I'm not making the same mistakes. So I guess I am learning from my parents what I should and should not be doing.

Tom, 12 When I'm married, I'll say, "Okay, let's compromise. This is what you want, and this is what I want. Let's see if we can get this to work if it's not too outrageous." And if it's too outrageous, I don't know how I'll handle it, but I doubt that it will be outrageous. I think that I would argue. If there is a marriage with no disagreements, call me.

Connie, 17 Is marriage worth it? I'm talking about all of the ups and downs and crappy things you go through all the time, and basically just living. I know that I'm really young right now, but I have a hard enough time knowing what I'm gonna wear tomorrow, let alone wondering what some stupid seventeen-year-old guy is thinking. Maybe it's just a cop-out for why I don't have a boyfriend, but at the same time I don't really want to be doing all of that. I am flunking precalculus. I don't need to be wondering what old Ted down the street is wondering about our relationship.

So that's why I'm not really concerned about that. But I do wanna know if they thought it was worth it—when these two get into fights or when they got divorced or when my stepdad and his previous wife got divorced. He said that he was completely and totally crushed after the divorce. He drank and smoked himself to almost death. He just wanted to die. I wanna know: Is it worth it?

I don't know very many happy marriages. I'm not saying I want Beaver Cleaver, but at the same time I don't wanna be fighting all the time and screaming at each other, and worrying about bills. It seems like life is stressful enough as it is.

Loretta, 21 I'm married. We knew that we wanted to get married, and we knew that there were problems that we have, residues left over from our parents' divorces and things that we need to work on. But we thought, "We can make this commitment to each other, and we can work on these things." We felt the thing that we learned from our parents' divorce is that you've gotta say things, you must talk. When you don't like something, you've gotta say it. And you've just gotta keep working on your relationship and never stop and never take it for granted.

Some people act like their wedding day is the climax, the goal. "I'm married. I'm entering into this wonderful world. The rest of my life is happily ever after." I think people take each other for granted when they get married because they just assume this other person is always gonna be there. You worked on this relationship and you've got them now. You got them to marry you.

We feel that as long as we work on it, we'll be okay. I get really frightened sometimes, and I get worried that it's gonna all fall apart. I don't wanna do that to us. And we wanna have kids, and I don't wanna do that to our kids. So it's hard, and my mom kind of accused us— "Well, your family fell apart, so you're going off and creating your own family"—and I know that was true. And I know that's a bad reason to get married, even as I know that's in part what we were both doing. Our wonderful family life had fallen apart. His parents' divorce really isn't over. Well, mine really isn't, either, in terms of the emotional piece.

They had gotten their divorce finalized on November first, and we got engaged on November third. I called Mom to tell her that we were engaged, and she said, "Oh. The divorce was final November first." So that was kind of weird, and she was real upset about me getting married—obviously because she feels I'm awfully young, and she was worried that I wouldn't finish my last year of school and issues like that. I myself think I'm too young, and I still sometimes think this probably wasn't the most sensible decision I've ever made, but I just feel like we know that, and we work on it.

Our wedding was kind of a tense thing, given all these issues going on. I was hoping to avoid some of the issues with my family. You know, my dad's side versus my mom's side kind of thing. I was letting him give me away, which really made me uncomfortable because I just don't believe in that, but I was doing it totally for him because I was like, "Well, I'm his only daughter. He won't get the opportunity to do this again." It's not like he has another, more traditional daughter. Initially I had thought about having both my parents give me away, but my mom felt uncomfortable with that because she didn't want to walk me down the aisle with my dad.

Nicole, 19 I guess in some ways the divorce made me grow up faster in how I deal with relationships. But I don't know that in general I grew up faster. I didn't feel like, "Now I have to go home and take care of my mom because Dad's not around," something I think a lot of people do. It did make me grow up a lot in how I viewed all types of relationships.

Roberta, 16 I've grown up being pretty independent because Mom was working and worrying about bills and everything else, and so I learned to be very independent. I don't depend on people.

Barb, 18 I can tell you that their divorce affected me more than anything you can imagine. It's really messed up how I see my future. How long ago was that? And I'm still crying about it, I'm still struggling with the stupid day-to-day crap.

Chloe, 7 Mom says marriage is good, but Dad says she's a liar. Dad says marriage is for stupid people, but Mom says Dad's a stupid person. I think they're both stupid and liars, and I will never get married because I won't be stupid.

Christina, 19 Some people have accused me of dating older men because I am looking for a father. I think there are things that people want out of a relationship. I sometimes felt that I wanted to be taken care of in a relationship, so I think I've looked for fathers to a certain extent.

Jane, 16 I don't know if it's worth it. I've been talking to a lot people about this stuff, and they're like, "Oh, yeah, we're happily married," but I don't see it. I'm not saying they can never get in a fight or that it has to be love and passion all the way, but I'm just saying that getting along would be nice.

Nick, 17 I think being divorced is better than being in a bad marriage. If the kid hears his parents arguing and fighting and screaming all the time, I think it changes all his views on marriage and relationships. He might even fear relationships when he's older. I kind of do now. I can't date the same girl for more than two months. I don't know if that has anything to do with the divorce, but maybe it does. My mom says the way I treat women is real bad. I don't think so. I just wanna get out of there. It's all kind of hard for me.

Nicole, 19 The divorce completely changed how I date. A lot of my friends think I have really weird dating habits, and the more I think about it, the more I realize that it's directly related to my parents.

It's not like I don't date. I do date quite often, but I'm extremely reluctant to get into anything serious. I love just having somebody to go to a movie with or go out to dinner with or something, but when it comes to a commitment, it's just like, "Oh, well, how much of a commitment is a commitment?" How long do these things really last if you say they last forever, but they might not really? I don't know.

I don't think I've ever been in love, and I think that's directly related to it. All of my friends are talking about "Oh, yeah, the first time I fell in love." "What? Okay." I'm extremely reluctant to get too emotionally attached to someone. I feel that even when you think something is forever, it can end, and so that really makes me standoffish. When it comes down to a real emotional commitment, when it gets to that point, I get so scared about it that I end it before it can get really deep into some emotional tie. I'm afraid of getting hurt by it like my parents were.

Jackie, 9 I'll build my own house to live in. Then we can all live there because it will be my house, and I'll be the boss.

Judi, 17 I see this guy Phil, and it seems like he's the perfect guy, but at the same time he's a lot older than me. There're people in their twenties, and I'm like, "Yeah, they're really cool and fun to talk to and everything, but how do you know, when things start getting bad, what's gonna happen?" That's really pessimistic, but I'm not gonna dedicate my entire life to some guy if the minute something bad happens, he runs, and I'm like, "Wait a minute. I was trusting here. I thought you were gonna be here, and you're not."

Barb, 18 I've only really dated two people. One was someone that I really didn't care much about. The other one began after my dad called me at school. He called me up drunk and told me that he just got divorced from his second wife. He was telling me all these details. He said, "I'm sorry. I'm a little drunk." And I was crying silently, trying to think, trying to listen, and he talked and talked. Finally, when he hung up, I completely lost it. I was bawling, feeling so much of his pain, feeling so sad that he had to talk to me about it. There were so many different facets, so many different perspectives. I was feeling all this different pain.

And he was there, this one boy was there to comfort me. Then we were very close, twenty-four-seven—you know, spending twenty-four hours, seven days a week together—for about two years, but he himself had a very bad family life. His parents weren't divorced, but that's just because the father wouldn't let them. It was hellish at home.

When he and I ended it, it was a very, very painful breakup for me, and I can tell you honestly I'm still reeling from it. It just happened this summer, which was weird because this summer was the first summer that I spent with Dad's new wife and the new stepson. So it was a lot of new things happening this summer.

Robin, 19 I think it'll take a lot for me to get married just because I've been through all of that once with my parents. No sense doing it over. I don't know what I would do. Hopefully I'll try to be normal about it. But I definitely wouldn't be the way my parents were. I'd make my own mistakes, but I wouldn't make the same ones they did. Mine will probably be stupid, too, but I wouldn't be that stupid. I wouldn't talk about the other one. I wouldn't try to make my kids think the other one was bad, which both of them did. That was a bad idea. I don't know what else I would do, but I wouldn't do that.

Jamal, 20 You have to let the person grow. My mom had just gotten a job, and her life had started up again. She had raised me, so she got a job. My father couldn't deal with that. You need to let that person grow up. I guess that's the key. Be willing to accept the person and the changes that are gonna come with them. And then don't have financial problems.

Loretta, 21 My fiancé would get angry, and I couldn't see it coming. I don't know how much that was me deluding myself, but I would then react exactly the same way I did to my dad even though my fiancé wasn't angry like that. He was rational about his anger. He was yelling, but he wasn't going insane and he wasn't saying nasty things. But I still would really freak out. I would hide in the closet and cry for hours and hours after work, and he would feel really bad. He'd be standing outside the closet saying, "Are you gonna come out? Can I come in? I'm sorry." It was pretty bad.

We're living with another couple because that was the best move financially for right now. I'm sure they were pretty shocked about the goings on, all this yelling and screaming and this ruckus all the time. They felt we shouldn't be getting married. That was their conclusion.

It was really rough. I can't even remember the things we fought over. They were dumb things, but I would get really, really upset. And whenever I thought he was unhappy with me, I was just a mess. I wasn't handling it well. Normally I can fight with people, but it's not like that. It was really devastating to me. He would get angry, and it would be like, "Oh, are you gonna turn into my dad someday? Maybe I shouldn't be marrying you."

Charlotte, 18 I think I've learned a lot of bad things. I've learned that if someone isn't aware of your needs, that's fine. Force them into whatever you want in a relationship. So now I tend to be like, "That's wrong. I'm not gonna let myself get into a trap like that." But I've been around it so long, it's still very natural. It becomes part of the way you deal with things. If you really think about it, it's not right.

Roberta, 16 I don't want to get married at this point. I don't want to put my kids through what I've had to go through, like "What am I supposed to call this stepguy, 'Dad' or 'Harry'?" Or "Where's my dad?"

In fifth grade the teacher said, "Most of your parents are married, right? Raise your hand if your parents are married." And there were four of "us" in the class. There were all these raised hands over our heads, and us four were like, "Oh." And I don't want my kids to have to go through that.

I don't know a happy marriage. Seriously, I don't know anyone who's happily married. I don't know if they're actually happily married or just tolerating each other or if they're together because they're just afraid of being alone.

Kelly, 18 One of my closest friends, once she gets into a relationship, she sticks with it, and she is with it for two years at a time. She's only had a few relationships, but what she has had has been extremely concentrated and serious and long-lasting and emotionally tied.

With me, I've had three dozen relationships, but they've all been a couple of weeks to a couple of months at a time, and as soon as they start to get serious, I get scared and back off. I pull away from people easily, though I've always been an extremely outgoing person. And I've never had a problem with sex. Of all those guys, nobody's ever complained. I really have no problem meeting people or talking to people, but then when it comes down to real ties, I have a hard time knowing how serious I can get with somebody and how much I can trust somebody. I think that really affects me a lot, and the older I get, the more I realize that's coming from what happened with my parents. It's not just something that's strange about me.

Christina, 19 I don't want to relive my mom's life. I think that's a fear I have.

Charlotte, 18 In relationships that I've had, I realized the position I'd always been in, and I said to myself, "This is not gonna do it. I can't continue to do this."

Jamal, 20 They started off in love, but I guess they just grew out of it. A lot of my father is part of me. He'll nitpick, gripe, bitch about everything, and I'll do the same thing, the same damn thing. I want to get married, but I probably won't. Well, maybe when I'm financially stable. When I get rich, I'll get married. I've seen what wealth does.

You never argue. It's just nice when you don't have to worry about money. At least that's what I think. I want to have, maybe, six or seven kids. Brothers and sisters help each other a lot.

Cassandra, 19 I'll have kids. I'm not going to have many. One or two. I hope that when I have my children, I am as good a mother as my mom was to me. She's really a great mom, and she did a great job, I think. I'm kind of plugging myself here. I think she really did well to help me form my mind and my own opinions, and we get along great. From my dad I have stubbornness like you would not believe. If I put my stubbornness on other adults, that doesn't bother me because most people know how I am and they're just like, "She's being stubborn." But I hope when I have children that I'm not as stubborn with them. I hope it's something I can block off from my children.

Barb, 18 I don't wanna have children. Palm readers have told me time and time again, "You're gonna get divorced. Whoa, boy, look at that divorce line." I mean anything, be it tarot cards or whatever, people have always told me, "No matter what, you're gonna get divorced." And I know it, too. If I ever got married, I would get divorced because I don't think I would enjoy marriage. I don't think I could see the benefits of it, and I don't see the benefits of having children. I can see more easily that things would get out of control with children than I can see having children that are well raised and behaving.

I don't want to have children who will experience the same kind of emotional stress that I have, that I go through to this day. I just can't see it. I've never wanted to have children, and I've never wanted to have a marriage.

Roberta, 16 I'm not saying I don't wanna have kids, but at the same time I don't know if I want kids because I hate kids. Mom says it's different when you have your own, but I had to drive my little half-brother and half-sister to McDonald's because it is like I am their mom. It's been that way since I was ten. I've been there through everything.

Mom went back and got her master's degree, and it was hell. I put the kids to bed, I cooked dinner, I walked them to school, I did everything. I was their mom, and I'm resentful of that.

I've definitely had kids, which is the best form of birth control you'll ever find in your life, spending an afternoon with them. I have some friends who come over sometimes, and Mom's like, "You know what? We're gonna practice birth control today! Safe sex! You're all spending the day with my little kids." This isn't to say I don't love them to death, because I totally do. I would do anything for them, but at the same time kids are just so needy and whiny, and they're just, "Me! Me! Me!"

Jewel, 18 It's so much harder on the kids than it is on the parents because a relationship can split, and you're like, "Okay, this guy's a jerk," or "This girl is a jerk," and you can go on with your life. But for the kids, that's their dad or their mother, and it's so much harder for them. The parents often don't consider that aspect of the divorce.

It's a wonder. Why do people even ask why our generation acts like we do? People don't care anymore. Girls go out and get pregnant when they're fourteen years old because they don't know what real relationships are. When you see your parents cheating on each other or you see your parents fighting or you see your parents hitting each other all the time, then why on earth would you ever want a relationship with somebody else? If you're never given that kind of model, then you're not gonna do it. So these people go out and they do drugs and they have sex and they do all these other things.

Christina, 19 I don't want to raise a kid on my own. A lot of times I'm afraid that I'll be in my forties and have regrets. You could say that I don't have a model of a successful relationship to go on. My mom's really happy in some ways. She's been able to make all the decisions in her life. She was dating a guy. It was real serious. They were living together. Last year she bought a purple Toyota, and it's a stormy color, and his first response was "Men don't drive in purple cars," and she was like, "Okay, drive yourself then."

It's kind of nice not having someone saying, "Why did you pick that color, and why do you want to rearrange the garden that way? Are you sure that's the right thing to do?" In a lot of ways she doesn't have to compromise with anybody. She's happy about that.

Vanessa, 17 My brother was raised without his dad around, and he had a really hard time with that. So did I, but not quite as much because it's girls and moms, and boys and dads, you know? I'm sure it really pissed him off that with Scouts and, whatever it's called, the pine-box derby thing where you have to make that car, he'd have one of Mom's friends help him make it. Everyone else's dads are like, "Yeah!" It just seems like the divorce thing is a lose-lose situation. It's hard.

Nicole, 19 I don't know that my brother will get married. My brother has internalized this a lot differently than I have, and I think I realized why I'm so standoffish with relationships. I think he has realized that he has a problem with it, but he isn't really willing to deal with it, so he just says, "Well, I probably won't get married. I just won't have kids. I won't get into that. I'll just stay with my own self. I wanna keep my own identity. I don't wanna get into that."

I think it has affected him in that way a lot more. I'll probably marry someday, but I think it will take a lot. I think before I marry anybody, it would take years of knowing them. It makes it difficult on me, but I think in the long run that will be much better. Now when I just want to be able to date and have fun and not worry about things like that, I do worry about them because of the divorce. I'm not going to be as prone to getting into a relationship that's going to end.

Christina, 19 In some ways I know in my heart that I really want to be married. I want to have a lasting, permanent relationship. I do not want to be married just to be married and have kids. In a way I don't want to have kids, 'cause I don't want to drag anybody through what I had.

Ruby, 20 I'm not really sure it would have been different if my parents had stayed together. Maybe I wouldn't have been so scared about commitment because I would have seen that their commitment lasted, but I probably still would have been scared because I'm sure that by now I would have realized the magnitude of how much they didn't get along and how strained and tense everything was between the two of them. I would have carried that into my relationships. It might have affected me differently, but I'm sure that their relationship would still be affecting how I look at relationships a lot.

Marvin, 19 I can't imagine myself getting married, but I think I certainly would try.

Nicole, 19 I think I'm probably so picky about everything and so tentative about getting into anything seriously because I don't want to get into anything like a controlling relationship. I'm not willing to lose myself, and I'm not willing to compromise myself. I am willing to start up a new identity with someone or to start a relationship that has good things come out of it. I'm willing to give a lot of myself, but I'm not willing to give up myself. I have to have my own identity.

Roberta, 16 I don't know if it's true you marry your dad or your

brother. I'm definitely not getting married if I marry the brother. So I
don't know what exactly I'm supposed to be looking for.

Wayne, 17 I'm not gonna be the same as my dad, and whoever I
marry is not gonna be the same as my mom. I think all relationships
are different, you know? But to say that I'm not gonna get married
now because my parents got divorced? Nah.

Sixteen

MY OWN MARRIAGE: Would I Get A Divorce?

Having been through a divorce themselves, many of these children have strong feelings about how they would confront the issue down the road.

Roberta, 16 I would not stick around a bad marriage. I find faults in guys quicker than they realize they have these faults, and I'm not the kind of person who's gonna sit there and take something over and over. I had a couple of friends like that, and I just don't understand. They get mad because I don't support them. "Why are you there? Why do you let your stupid high school boyfriend treat you like this? What are you gonna do? Are you gonna get married to some abusive guy?" "Oh, he doesn't mean to beat me. He's really upset about it." I have a friend who's been hit a couple of times by her boyfriend, and I just have no patience for that.

Loretta, 21 Divorce is just not an option for me. I think if you make it an option, you're not really married. Marriage is a lifelong commitment. I think that's why the tension before we got married was so bad. If we get divorced, it is not because I want us to get divorced. It's because he is the one who said, "No more." I mean, I will fight with him and yell at him until I'm blue in the face, but I will not divorce. It isn't an option because it's just dissolving a family. You've created this family, and you're just gonna destroy it with a divorce.

Charlotte, 18 If I were married and we were having trouble, I think I'd try to see if it could be remedied. If it couldn't, I would get a divorce, because it doesn't help anyone to stay in a situation like that, especially if it's just not gonna be remedied. I think a relationship takes a lot of work, and you have to be willing to do that. You have to be willing to try to identify what the problems are and try to fix them and try to see if you can compromise. I definitely would try counseling.

Riza, 18 I'm definitely gonna get married. I'm definitely gonna have kids. And I'm definitely going to be the first member of my family not to get divorced. That's my goal in life, because one thing that really bothers me—and I really get on a little soapbox on this one—is how acceptable divorce has become. Marriage used to be a very stable institution. They'd go in there and they're like, "Okay, this is marriage, and this is till death do us part." And now it's "Till our first conflict arises."

Or people will do things like get married and say, "I'm marrying my first wife." Your first? And how many others are you going to have? They see it as a longer form of dating, which it isn't and shouldn't be. People have gotten so used to moving around in jobs and houses, nobody stays in the same house all their life anymore. I never lived in the same place. I was constantly moving around. I do have friends that say, "Yeah, well I was born here and have lived here all my life, and now I need to get out." But those are just a few, and those have the parents who have been together all their life, and those are people that I kind of look at as the exception now instead of the norm. Which just really bugs me. What's wrong with that?

Tom, 12 My mom says, "Don't get married to get divorced." I've read books, graphs, and things, and like fifty percent of married people get divorced. I say to myself, "If that ever happens, I'm gonna kind of expect it."

Loretta, 21 I'm not scared. I'm scared of things that I can't see that might happen, but if I am committed to working and if I am committed to sharing my feelings and not keeping things from my husband, then I've done the best I can possibly do, and as long as he does that, too, it's gonna be okay.

And I'm willing to do whatever it takes. If we get to the stage where we can't talk to each other, I'm willing to go for counseling. We actually thought about going for premarital counseling or just counseling in general because we're worried about the effect our parents' divorce is having on our own relationship. But we haven't really gotten our act together, and we don't have much money. I can see us doing that in a couple years maybe even though nothing's wrong, but just to make sure there aren't underlying issues that are festering.

Elliot, 11 If I got a divorce, it would probably be at an early age or a very late age, since in the middle, marriage is like a jigsaw puzzle that you really haven't finished. You haven't seen the whole facts of life. But then if you're older, if you get a divorce late in life—I'm talking about maybe eighty, not fifty, but like really late—then your jigsaw is basically done. My parents were in between.

Riza, 18 To some extent it's good to be able to change. If you're in a bad marriage, get out of it, get out of it fast, and do it early, but don't get into a marriage where you're not going to mean it.

Nicole, 19 I think I'd be quick to get a divorce. I'm hoping I won't get into that situation because I'm going to be so picky. But I think if I got into the situation where I was faced with that, and I thought, "I just can't live with this person anymore"—if it ever came down to that point where I was wondering about it—I think I would do it. Whereas people who haven't been through it yet, they would worry about "Will this hurt the kids too much? Will I be able to make it afterward? Will

180

they still be able to go to college if they don't have both of us together and the two incomes?'' Things like that.

I think I've seen that it's not the best thing, but it's also not the best thing to make the kids live in the home when everything is upset and nobody's getting along. If it got to the point where I felt like divorce was what was needed to be done, I don't think I would be as reluctant to do it as some people would, because I think I'd realize that just drawing it out and pretending the trouble wasn't there when it certainly was, that's just as bad.

I think I'd be reluctant to come to that conclusion, but if I ever came to the conclusion that that was necessary, that that was the only way to get out of it, I don't think I'd stay in it once I was thinking that it was done.

Maria, 15 Divorce is very selfish. Divorce is two people who have said, "Sorry, it's easier for me to get a new relationship than fix this one." But you're not dating, you're married. This is a commitment. You decided to make this family, and you can't just walk away from it. It just isn't right. It's not right for anyone.

Riza, 18 I have this goal. I haven't actually planned it out yet, but I think I'm just going to be extra doubly careful before I actually get into a marriage. I definitely want to get married, but I don't want to rush into one, because I see couples that are getting married because the woman's pregnant, which I think is a really stupid excuse to get married. Or because they've been dating for six months, and she decided, "Okay, he's the one." I just look at the people, and I decide that they're either very lucky or just plain stupid. If it's going to work out, then you can wait a little while, and it will work out just as well if not better.

So I'm definitely going to wait. I'll live with the guy for a while and get used to interacting in as marriage-like a way as possible. I'm aware that none of my parents planned to get divorced. It's not the thing you put in your plans for "what I'm going to do when I grow up." But I think I can say they weren't as careful. Not that my dad could have expected that his second wife would leave. I mean, I'm not blaming anybody for this, but I'm saying that if people are a little more careful, then there's a smaller chance of divorce happening.

Christina, 19 It's not easy raising a kid by yourself. It's sure not easy raising two kids by yourself. There are some things about it that are easier, though. There is nobody else gainsaying your opinion. I mean, you have to make a decision, but at the same time you get to make a decision. You don't have to compromise with anyone else.

Tom, 12 I would tell my kids if there was trouble in the marriage, if they were old enough. I would say eight or nine. I would tell them the whole dreaded thing. But if they were five, six, seven, I would say, "We're getting a divorce," and I'd tell a little white lie. Below that age I would say, "I will tell you later," and I would just keep on procrastinating until they are maybe five or six.

Riza, 18 My dad's parents, they waited until all the kids were grown up and out of the house, or at least getting out of the house, when they got divorced. They knew they were staying together for the kids. It was so stupid. I heard the stories from my dad; the older I got, the freer he felt to tell me these things. He'd tell me all this stuff about fights that went on in their house—doors slamming, yelling, and just other awful stuff. And these parents are supposedly staying together for the kids?

Seventeen

COPING: How Do I Handle This?

Children have diverse ways of coping with divorce and its
aftermath, and they are happy to give advice to others who
are going through it. Sometimes what they advise is what they
have done themselves, and sometimes it is what they wish they
had done.

One general pattern is that males are much more likely to
try to ignore the situation and the associated emotions. This is
certainly not exclusive to children. Men and boys are simply
less likely to seek help than are woman and girls, whether the
help is for a major crisis or road directions.

Coping with divorce does not have a cutoff age. There is no
time limit for how long it takes to get over it. When adults
become impatient with children and young adults because the
pain or issues from the divorce remain visible, that
impatience can send the victim into retreat from facing the
problem, lengthening and complicating the grieving process
and the period of adjustment. There's no hurry, and the
child must not be made to feel guilty for moving at his or
her own pace.

Christina, 19 It gets better. A really hard thing to say to a kid who
says, "My parents are getting a divorce," is that in the end it's a good
thing.

But you also have a right to say to the kid, "Yeah, I have a problem with my dad." That doesn't mean I don't need to try to have a relationship with him, but sometimes it's hard to. Society doesn't notice that. I mean, "honor thy mother and father" is one of the Ten Commandments, and you don't really get to say, "To hell with you, Dad." Instead it's "Well, you know, you should get over it. You're practically an adult now." No, you don't get over it. You're still angry about it. It still affects your life, and it is still something.

Nicole, 19 I think my brother took the pain inside himself. He'd go off and hang out with his friends a lot, but I know that he didn't talk with them about it. He was dealing with it on his own without anybody else, and I think that's just the way some people have to deal with it. I think he wouldn't have known what to do if somebody had come to him and said, "Hey, let's sit down and talk about this." If it were, say, my mom's best friend, I think he would have felt like he was going against my dad, being a traitor. So I think you have to figure out what type of a person they are and then help them out accordingly.

Tom, 12 The therapist I see, I tell him whatever happened, and then at the end he'll scribble something in his notebook, really short, and say, "Okay, that's it for today." I like him. It's just the helpfulness that I get from him that feels good.

Robin, 19 I wonder about my sanity sometimes. I don't really remember things in the right order. Like if I remember things, I remember them all messed up. I think I was trying to not be conscious, and I succeeded far too well, 'cause I don't remember a lot of stuff.

Elliot, 11 Sometimes you do need things to help get you through, like spending time with my dog or talking to a true best friend or, even better, an adult. My brother and sister helped, but I'm talking about other people that understand it.

Riza, 18 What I'd usually do is accept these things that happen as fact, like don't cry over spilt milk. Be resilient. I had to become that way. I regret it sometimes. In high school my best friend was the kind of person who could get emotional about things. If anything bothered her, she'd just cry it out. Sometimes it was easy to make fun of. But other times I got really jealous because for years, even now, I've found it very difficult to cry. I just physically couldn't. Lots of times I've tried to cry, and it just won't work. I'll just take in the facts and say, "Okay, that's the way it is, and I have to accept it." I'll get real rational.

When I was little, I'd cry if I was angry sometimes. Sometimes I'd cry if I was in physical pain, but it slowed down to a complete halt. At some point I just didn't cry at all. I'd get hit really hard, and I'd just go, "Ow." I couldn't cry anymore. Recently I've been trying to break all that down. I say, "Okay, I have to get more in touch with this side of me again." It is not easy.

Ted, 12 They said, "Come downstairs." Then they said, "We're splitting up. Dad's moving out tomorrow." What could I do? I started to cry. I cried for a long time. But I used to cry a lot when I listened to them fight at night, and I haven't cried about my mom and dad since they told us that they were getting a divorce. I just try not to think about it now. My sisters like to talk about it, but I don't want to. I think girls like to talk about it, and boys like to forget about it. Just one more way that girls are kinda dumb.

Heather, 6 My friend's mom and dad are getting a divorce, and she was scared about it, so I told her, "Don't worry. It isn't you're fault. You're still going to have a good life."

Wayne, 17 There was my grandma, but I couldn't talk to her about my problems with the divorce because no matter how I ever said anything, she would always take my mom's side. She would always criticize me—I mean, in a good way. That's the thing. But it made me mad. She's one of those old religious fanatics, like, "God wouldn't like you doing this," and stuff like that. I mean, I'm Catholic now, but she goes too far with it.

Roland, 19 There's a part of you that feels "You can never make it up to me" and never lets them. I never really gave up, but it's been very hard to forgive my mom. And I don't want to be a hateful person, and I don't want to hate my mom.

Ken, 13 I'm not really jealous of my friends who have parents who aren't divorced. It's no big deal to be divorced. If I get to know a new kid in school, they're like, "Your parents are divorced?" I'm like, "Yeah. You didn't know that?" It's kind of like kids who don't know I have contact lenses because they've just met me. They're like, "You have contacts?" Yeah, no big deal.

Martin, 18 If my friend's parents get a divorce, I'll tell him he has to deal with it in his own way. Or I'd just say, "If you need to talk, talk." There's really no patented formula for dealing with parents' divorce. If you can find an easy way, I'm sure you'll make a lot of money.

Carie, 15 When we moved, a lot of kids' parents here were divorced, and I joined the Rainbows group, which did divorce. I guess that helped. You knew that there were other kids whose parents were divorced. But you just have to stick through it. Things will never go back to the way they were. Things will always be different. Things seem really bad at first, and then they eventually get better, no matter how awful they seem.

Barb, 18 The divorce has been one of the strongest things in my life. My parents became so much in the forefront in my life, so primary.

186

It was kind of a screwed-up experience to go through. I cried a lot, and I vented this all out on my best friend, and she listened. She tried to calm me down a little bit. The good thing about her is she's not one to give all this advice. She's a really good listener. That's one thing I really appreciate about her. That kept me going.

And you know what? When I mention to my parents these days that I was crying and all that, they are completely surprised. They have no idea. They thought I was a very well adjusted, very confident kid because I can present that. When I'm crying in my room, when I'm breaking down, crying on the phone to my friend, I'm not doing this on a phone in the kitchen, I'm doing this on a phone in the bedroom, with the door closed. The rest of the time, all the kids, the people I knew, they all knew me as very friendly. When my best friend left on vacation this summer, all this hell happened, and I was left with no one to speak to. This one friend that I had to resort to talking to, I had to start from square one, and she said, "Oh, my God. I had no idea."

But I was surprised that my parents had no idea. They still cannot believe that I am emotionally fragile, that I crumble a lot, and they cannot accept it. Whenever I exhibit any characteristics contrary to a sort of happy image, they're like, "This is not the Barb I know. This is not the Barb that we watched grow up. This is not the same Barb." And I told them over and over again, "This is the Barb that was in high school, the same Barb that was in junior high. You just didn't know."

I am less patient now with putting up false fronts. I can't do it so much anymore, making white lies. It involves a lot of energy, and it's almost schizophrenic, like you're two different people.

I took solace in it in high school because people thought I was carefree, that things were pretty good with me. Some people from high school would describe me as always having a smile on my face. Very ironic, because I cried so much.

Since I came to college, I couldn't start the introductions anymore this way. I don't know why. I just couldn't. I'm now viewed here at college as reclusive. I tried to hide myself away. I do have a group of friends, but I don't tell them any of this. I don't want to explain, and it's really none of their business, honestly.

But the thing is, the reason I don't go out and make a lot of new friends is just that I don't want to start with these damn white lies again. If there's a mood swing or someone asks, "Why are you feeling bad?"—if they caught me on a bad day or something—I'd have to make up a white lie. I can't do that anymore. It's confusing, it's annoying, and it's false. The better thing is to keep the one or two friends that I have who know the private things about me, all the bits and pieces. I tell each of them, selectively, certain parts that I think they would be able to handle. Then I swear them to secrecy. So even though these friends may collectively be friends with each other and talk to each other, they don't talk to each other regarding me.

That one best friend of mine, she knows everything. She's the only one. Everyone else that I have as a confidante knows this much, that much. And when I'm talking to this person, I have to remember this person knows this much because otherwise you have to start from "Well, it's a very complicated story. Let's start from square one," and then it kind of sounds like you're pretty much a basket case, and it seems very odd. But it's not odd, and it's very much real.

Wayne, 17 Don't let it get to your head.

Christina, 19 I don't define myself as a child of divorce but more as a child of a single mother, which is a different thing. It doesn't have any negative meaning, at least not to me.

Martin, 18 I didn't really talk to anyone about my parents getting divorced. When I did, it was usually to show off, like, "Yeah, my parents are getting divorced," just to dig for that attention. If somebody came to show off their soccer ball or something like that, I'd say, "Yeah? Well, my parents are getting divorced." Make yourself feel like the center of the universe again. It's a thing you do when you're a kid, like whoever has the biggest toy to show off or the biggest thing to talk about. It fits, though, because sometimes marriage is political. Some people stay together just for appearances.

Sally, 6 My dad gave me a doll for Christmas, and I named the doll Ellen, my mother's name. I can talk to the doll about anything.

Carmen, 16 When I was living with my dad, my mom sent me this doll, and I named it Loaf of Bread. It's the most hideous thing you ever saw in your life. I have it upstairs. Either she had made it or someone she knew had made it. I loved it, but when you look at it, it's really gross now because it's hand-sewn and stuff. If I was mad at my dad or at my mom, I'd lock it in the closet or in the bathroom. When I look back now, I was only four, and how angry is that?

And I wanted to run away. I had this yellow plasticky raincoat-material bag. And I kept it packed with books and pennies and stuff. I was going to run away, and every night I found some excuse as to why I couldn't. I can't remember where I was going to run to or what I was going to do, but I guess I just wanted to get out of there. It was weird because I don't really even remember anything else from then—just those two things, Loaf of Bread and my little bag.

Ted, 12 My friend's parents are getting a divorce. I told him, "It won't be fun. You won't like it. But after a while you'll get used to it."

Nick, 17 After the divorce, my sister and I were always home alone during the summers and the school breaks, and my mom was working and couldn't take off work. She needed the money, so we were always home alone, and we kind of had to raise ourselves—not really raise ourselves, but we were always pretty much on our own.

I guess doing that taught me to make my own decisions early. I don't want to blame anything in my life on someone or something, but I think maybe I don't listen to anyone because I had to be on my own, by myself, for a long time. I just never really liked listening to anyone. Everyone's telling me stuff, and I just believe what I want to believe and don't really pay attention to anyone else.

Robin, 19 I think that I was told a lot of things that weren't true, and, of course, I believed them all.

Ken, 13 When a friend of mine's parents are getting a divorce, I tell him it won't be as hard as you expect it to be. Just go on with your life, call friends, get out of the house, go on with a normal life. Don't pay attention that your parents are divorced because in the end it'll probably be easier for you if you just stick to what you're doing. Just have fun. Pretty much be a kid. Ignore it as much as you can.

Christina, 19 In college there's a lot of defensive sarcasm and humor, but I think in a lot of ways it's our coping mechanism. "Hey, that's just the way it is." Because you get really sick of crying. We are all so busy being logical in college, we do try to laugh it off a lot. But it ain't always so easy. Like with me and my sister, it's been weird about my dad. She feels she tries a lot harder to have a relationship with my dad than I do, and I think she doesn't realize how hard it is for me.

Wayne, 17 The thing was, my parents didn't really care what I thought about it. It didn't seem like it anyway. They didn't talk to me in the sense that, like, "You know, we should tell him and see how he really feels about this." I'm sure my mom asked me how I felt, and I'm sure I was probably so mad at the time. I was like, "Whatever. If you guys are gonna be like that, why don't you just go to hell."

The type of angry behavior Ted describes is not uncommon during and shortly after a divorce. The fury has to come out somewhere.

Ted, 12 We had to go see a counselor after my parents got their separation but not because of that. It was because my brother and I started fighting really bad, and they thought I had hurt him.

Nicole, 19 I don't know that I ever felt like I was part of the problem. I think they made that clear right off the bat that this was just between them. It was going to affect us, but it was not because of us, which helps a lot. Sometimes I felt I was part of the problem when it came down to what happened because of the divorce and after the divorce, and what was happening between them, how things didn't die down between them afterward, and how they'd still get in arguments when they'd have to call each other. I felt like, "Well, gosh, if I didn't want to take this acting class and didn't need the hundred bucks for it, then they wouldn't have to be talking on the phone about 'Are you gonna pay that or am I?'"

Sometimes I felt like, "Well, I'm just not gonna deal with this. I'm not going to take that class this year because I don't wanna have to deal with the fight," but I don't think I ever felt like I was at fault about the divorce itself. Other adults I'd talk with helped a lot on that, too. I don't think they realize how much those people helped us get through that, and I think my dad resents the people I talk to about it who were friends of my mom's or who were from our church who sided with my mom. But that's the way I got through it. I would have had a much more difficult time otherwise. It's a necessity to have people who will let you know what's going on and not treat you as just a kid and advise you not to worry about it.

Tom, 12 Kids should ask questions. Ask about what's on your mind. If you don't know, ask. Your parents will probably be straightforward with you. Don't overdo it. Don't take things so emotionally and then say, "I'm gonna die in five years. I'm gonna do something bad," or something like that. If you do, eventually someday it's gonna get so tight in your brain that you won't even remember they were married. Ask your parents or a relative, an aunt or uncle. I was too naive. One time I asked them, "Would you have been straightforward with me?" and Mom said yes. She had to pause for a second before she answered.

Nick, 17 Don't think it's your fault. It's never the kid's fault.

Wayne, 17 I didn't really ever talk about my family problems with anybody. I usually talked with one of my good friends. We always talk about other things, but the divorce is just something I never talked about.

Robin, 19 Last year a friend was crying all night about something. I was upset, too, and I was like, "My mom is disowning me." And she didn't even know my parents were divorced. We've been friends since last year. She's like, "You never, ever talk about your family." I'm like, "I know." My roommate's like, "We know. She's getting over that." Give me a break. I'm trying.

Nicole, 19 I guess it was good that I had a lot of adult influences. My mom's best friend's a pastor. I talked to her a lot. Dad always figured that she was part of the reason they broke up. I don't think that the divorce had anything to do with her. It was just that she helped Mom realize that there was life outside of taking care of your husband.

My fifth grade teacher is still my favorite teacher I ever had, and he was the one I had when I was going through the separation. He was somebody else that I could go and talk to, and I had a really close best friend at the time. I'd hang out with her a lot and try to get out of the house. It helped.

I've always been a talker and someone who really needs to contemplate things. I can't just let something go or let something happen on its own and then deal with it later. I'm usually fine with the changes that happen, but I need to be able to think about them in my own way to be able to come to terms with them. So that gave me the opportunity to do so, to have people to talk to about it.

The adults, especially, were willing to listen. I think a lot of times when you see this little fifth grader come up to you, saying, "I don't know what's going on with my parents," the idea is just to say, "It'll be okay. Don't worry about it," and not let them know what's actually going on. I say, let them know. "Well, yeah, your dad's not coming back to the house anymore. This is the way it's gonna be," and don't sugarcoat it. Don't say, "Well, maybe they'll get back together," because, looking back on it, there was no way they were going to get back together.

In my case it was good having people who were enough on the inside of the issue to know what was going on but not so much on the inside that they were extremely biased one way or the other. But the further you get into the divorce, you find that everybody moves to one side or the other. Unfortunately, there are a lot of broken friendships because of divorce, because of people taking sides, especially when the divorce gets ugly.

Christina, 19 The thing with divorce is that it is so common, people tend to normalize it or dismiss it as much less than what it actually means.

Elliot, 11 The first few years, all you want to do is get back at them, or you're sad. It's pretty rocky, and you don't know what you're doing. It's like having half a map. You don't know where you're going to end up.

Eighteen

THE AFTERMATH: I'm Different Now

Children of divorce, even those who would rather look the
other way when it comes to their own pain, will usually admit
that the divorce has changed them in some way even if the
divorce occurred when they were babies.

Martin, 18 The divorce didn't change me, value-wise. Mostly it helped deaden me to the emotional impact of events. Like if the dog got run over, I probably wouldn't be as upset.

Robin, 19 The few kids who I've talked to about divorce—it's not good to say, but I think they're more okay with it than I am. I've never talked to anyone who was upset about it, so that would be a different situation, I'm sure. I've been a lifeguard at the pool for six years. It's a small town. I know all the kids, and they're cool. But I know one kid, and it's just like, "This is my stepbrother," and I'm like, "Hi," and it bothers me. Another shitty situation I'm in. It makes me feel bad. Kids will be playing together with their stepsisters and stepbrothers at the pool, and I'll just be like, "That's cool," but it'll make me mad, and no one else is mad about it.

Tom, 12 We sort of got off the mainstream. Everyone else's parents who were divorced were friends with the other parent, both of them getting along. Then it became: If we went to some event, my dad would be on one side and my mom on the other, watching. They literally had to be like that, with my mom on one side of a place and my dad on the other. They couldn't be within a certain distance of each other for something like six months after they divorced. Six months, and they couldn't be within a certain distance of each other. Do you believe that?

Christina, 19 I think my self-confidence comes from the fact that I grew up in a single parent family where there was no message other than "You can do anything you want." There was no sense of "Women are different from men." There was just women. It's funny—on a Girl Scout cookie box it says that it's important for women to spend time in the support of an all-female environment during adolescent years. Well, I did. I grew up in a supportive all-female environment.

Loretta expresses beautifully the dilemma that so many children and young adults find themselves in. No matter what age a child was when her parents divorced or what the circumstances were or how long ago it happened, the ripples may continue to spread.

Loretta, 21 People, especially people whose parents haven't been divorced, think that because it happened when I was nineteen and because I was away at college and because I wasn't there in the home, it shouldn't be a big deal. Even my husband gets this way sometimes, because my parents had a smooth divorce. There wasn't a lot of contesting going on in court, but that doesn't mean it wasn't just as emotional, and it doesn't mean that I don't have my own issues to deal with whether I was there or not. It's still a problem for me, and I get angry when people think, "Oh, well, you should be fine now. It should be no big deal. You weren't even there." My brothers do that, too, and I know their experience was different.

But I just don't think it's fair when people think, "Well, this other divorce was really bad, so this person's experience was much worse." It doesn't matter. It affects everyone differently, and the experience is very painful. Last summer I was upset a lot, and I felt my roommates were judging me. Their parents are married, and they were going, "Your parents got divorced your sophomore year. You're going into your senior year now, and it's not like you're a kid. It's not like you had to deal with 'who am I gonna live with' and things like that. So why are you so upset over this? You must be really messed up."

It just makes me so angry because I feel it isn't my problem. I have every right to feel this way. And not only that, but my parents pulled me into this. This wasn't just about my parents breaking up. This was about my family breaking. And they can't possibly know what this feels like. Their families are together. This isn't a divorce, this is a family. You're divorcing a family, you're not divorcing just a person. I think even my dad had the wrong idea about that. He thought he was just divorcing a person, not breaking a family apart.

I wouldn't have expected myself to react in some of the ways that I did, and I honestly wouldn't have expected to be upset years later. Like I said, I think I'm fairly well over it now, but my husband could get angry at me tonight, and I could end up in the closet again crying.

Jody, 20 It seems like it should be all over and done with after eight years, but it's really not. I guess I feel weird being like "yeah, but . . ." because I'm twenty.

Sally, 6 I was two. I don't really remember it, but I feel bad and sad, because you really like your dad and mom. So I usually just cry because I get so sad and mad because my mom and dad are divorced.

Martin, 18 I'll probably drive my wife nuts, wanting to move every year and a half like we did. "Well, hon, I think we need a change of pace." We'll see.

Cassandra, 19 I used to be a very trusting person. But now I always double-think what I'm going to tell anybody and whether I should just keep it to myself. But I tell everything to my mom, absolutely everything. And this includes all my relationships, with any guy. Her and I, we're just open books. So she's definitely the person I trust most in my life. And then, I just kind of pick and choose everybody else.

Ziq, 13 What eventually happened is that they did Effective Ed at school. They were like, "Now raise your hand if you got divorced." In my first grade class, sixty people, there were three who raised their hands. Even that they would do this—that "raise your hand" thing— was terrible for me. Me and just one other boy and a girl raised our hands out of sixty kids. Just us three. But by fifth grade over half the class raised their hands. Good! Now they can feel it.

Dexter, 13 I used to like school a lot. Now since they got divorced, it's just okay. Really, I don't like anything that much anymore.

Loretta, 21 Your family is your whole life, your whole center, and to have that center fall apart is really something. I always had the confidence to go out and do things because my family was back there supporting me. Now, suddenly, in some sense they're not. I mean, I know that individually they still are, but it's still really devastating, and I think it would have devastated me even if I was much older, even if I had been over the stage of idealizing my parents. It still would have been this circle, this unit, that I relied on, and it's just not there anymore.

Christina, 19 A lot of people don't want to hear about your parents being divorced. They get sort of angry if they hear you talk about it all the time, like, "Your dad, yeah, yeah."

Have a little sympathy. I could go to my friend and say, "Yeah, yeah, your mom's dead. Get over it." But I wouldn't say that. To a certain extent, divorced parents are something like that, this delicate issue. I'm pretty comfortable with it and can laugh at it, but I still don't want people acting like I don't deserve to talk about it—and some people do. They have no concept of what it is like, and it's very hard for them to understand.

Natalie, 19 Sometimes I honestly wish my mom had died. I honestly thought it would have been better for all of us. People would have sympathy for us. People would have understood. They wouldn't have judged us.

Some people reacted in ways that I didn't want them to. I might tell my friends, "My mom did this. I'm upset. I need to talk to someone." They'd be like, "Oh, your mother, what a bitch," which is the last thing I wanted to hear from them. I wanted them to listen to me. I didn't want them to tell me what a bitch my mother was because that was a very painful realization, that she could be a bitch.

And there were days like that where I really, honestly wished she had died. Then there'd be only happy memories. I was scared of the idea of divorce when I was twelve, and I've never been scared of my parents dying. It never even occurred to me until the divorce.

Another thing is the length of time you get to feel bad. I think people accept and understand that when a parent dies, it may take you years to recover, and you're never gonna be the same person again. But with divorce, no one realizes that. No one acknowledges it.

Martin, 18 No matter what anybody says, divorce will always affect you more than most people realize. Divorce is one of those things that'll affect you for better or for worse, even though I might not admit it fully to myself.

But you can either deal with life creatively or apathetically. Either you ignore it or do something with it. Where am I on that scale? I'm not quite sure. In the gray area, maybe. I'll tell you later, twenty years from now, when you write the sequel: *"Divorce Kids, Part Two: The Revenge.* See how their kids treat them!"

Nineteen

REUNION FANTASY: Should They Still Be Together?

*Not all children wish their parents were still married, though
at the time of the divorce most children do have that fantasy.
As time passes, however, some maintain that fantasy, others
give it up, and some come to feel that a reunion would be the
last thing they would want to see.*

Fred, 9 I wish that my parents could be together without fighting
each other and that I could spend equal time with both of them and
that they'd be together. It would be dull if they never argued, I guess.
But I guess that is a good kind of dull.

Roberta, 16 I guess they were going to get back together at some
point. Or so they said. If they had told me that, I would have been like,
"Yay! My mom and dad are getting back together!" Looking back, I
don't see how they could have even said that. I don't know that they
ever saw each other. It was just "Hi, Gladys, I'm picking up the kids"
and "Bye, Gladys, I'm leaving now." I look at the two of them, and
they are completely opposite. And I've always wondered why. I never
even asked her, "What did you see in each other? What was it like
when you first started dating?" I know they met through their church.

Charlotte, 18 Should they stay together? No, absolutely not. They
think they should stay together, and it aggravates me because I don't

think they realize that it has a detrimental effect on me and my brother. That's the model relationship that we have, and it's a bad one. The message we get is that relationships are bad but we're supposed to just stay in and force ourselves to put up with it, and that's not true. It's not healthy for you to force yourself to stay in a relationship when you're not getting what you need. They've been in it for a long time, and the whole family's just like, "You've been doing this long enough. Just stop."

They said that it's not because of us that they are still together, and I don't think it is. I just think that they've been together for a long time, and I think they are people who never saw themselves as divorced. It was something you didn't do. It never crossed their minds as an option.

Nicole, 19 The advice I'd give to kids would be talk to your parents. I guess advice to parents would be don't stay in a relationship that's bad because of the kids. Don't figure that it's necessarily in the kids' interest, because it isn't always. In my case it was much better after the divorce. The house wasn't as tense as it had been. I could have a good relationship with each of them separately, but I didn't have to deal with the problems, and it ended up being a lot better for me once the divorce happened—a lot better than if they had stayed together and been fighting.

Riza, 18 I grew up without any real hostility toward their divorce. I wasn't ever really mad at them for getting divorced. In fact, I was very happy that they got divorced, thinking of all the pain I would have been put through growing up with fighting parents, if they had stayed together. This way I got the direct relationship with each parent, and I got the no-conflict. It was a really nice choice on their part.

Wayne, 17 Depending on how old the kid is, I think you'd have to ask him how he feels. "Is this a problem for you because we're having problems?" or something. You'd have to involve your children. If they don't ask, it's not fair, because they don't know how we feel, and then they do stuff. I would ask my kid what he felt like if I was in a marriage that wasn't going too well. I wouldn't just pretend that everything was okay if it wasn't. I would sit down and talk with my kid—have a family talk or something. Because to this day I think maybe they'd still be together if they had, and I wish they had.

Serena, 11 If I had three wishes, I'd ask for a thousand more wishes. Then I'd make every single wish be that my mom and dad would get back together and stay together forever—plus one wish for my dog, that he didn't die.

Jewel, 18 I'm ever so thankful that my parents got divorced because in the most crucial part of my life, when you're making decisions and forming your morals and forming your character, he was away. He was not sitting there going, "No, you can't do this. No, you can't think that." So it was a good time for my parents to get divorced, because otherwise I wouldn't be this strong-minded person that I am today.

Tom, 12 In the beginning, yes, I'd hope they'd stay together. I stopped hoping for that when my dad got married again. When it looked like Dad and his girlfriend were solid, I thought, "Mom and Dad, you're never gonna get married again," and every day Dad got closer to getting married, it got slimmer and slimmer and slimmer. Then the day that he got married, it bursted into nothing, and I turned that hope off.

Robin, 19 When I was a kid, I felt they were very immature. Like, "Try to work it out." I mean, sometimes you just can't. If it's not both people trying, then sometimes you really just can't.

Now I don't know. I definitely think they shouldn't have stayed together forever. They weren't really together anyway. I probably shouldn't even be here, because it was way bad before I came along. At least that's the way I see it. So many things you learn when you get older. When I was a kid, I tried everything you can think of to get them back together. The famous little "Dad, Mom misses you" and "Mom, Dad misses you."

But then they'd just get mad at me. Mom would be like, "Robin, stop. That's not true." I'm like, "Yes, it is." Dad would just be like, "I don't want you to talk about her," and I'd be like, "I can if I want." I probably didn't help.

But that's okay. I tried. It didn't work. I guess I just always thought they would get back together. I know it wasn't until after I was in high school before I gave that up. I remember at my eighth grade graduation, I was really upset because I was like, "Man, I always thought that by my graduation, my parents would be sitting together." But no, they definitely weren't.

Loretta, 21 Should they have stayed together? Oh, no, I don't delude myself. I wouldn't want them to, because he wasn't good to her. When I look at my brother and see that he is helping Mom in the kitchen, he is better off, and Mom's a better person, too. They got married when they were nineteen, right out of high school.

Certain things had always scared Mom. Driving out of town by herself, for one, and now she does. She's just gained so much more independence. Maybe they could've worked things out if they'd gone to counseling. At first I wished that they had.

Roberta, 16 One reason I'm glad they got divorced is that it has made me realize that life isn't this great, perfect, happy thing, that things can go wrong, but we do pick up the pieces and move on. It's made an impact on me. Even though they had to go through so much sorrow to do it, they still managed to move on. There's hope in life without 2.5 kids, a dog, and a driveway, with everything perfect.

I see now that you don't even have to maintain an image that everything's perfect. My parents getting divorced says to me, "Hey, I don't have to do that. I don't have to remain in a relationship that isn't good because society says it's bad if we break up." I've learned that I don't necessarily need a man—to get along in life. I can be independent, you know? I'm going to stand up for my beliefs. You can trust yourself, trust your gut to know "this isn't good. I don't like this. Get out." Your instinct is heightened.

Manolo, 7 Every night I pray over and over and over and over until I fall asleep that my dad will come back to the house. I know I see him a lot, but I feel scared when I think that he will never live here again. I feel like crying now to talk about it. I'm all done talking now.

Heather, 6 It's okay that they got a divorce because my grandmother helps out a lot. But it's better to be married because you can make more money or your mom can stay home with you. I have to go to after-care or else my mom couldn't make any money and go to work. It's nice there. I know everybody, so I like it.

Nick, 17 I used to wish they stayed together when I was little. I really missed my dad a lot. I was in the Cub Scouts, and every time there were father and son things, I always got some surrogate father from the neighborhood. I mean, it was cool, the guy was real nice, but it's just not the same when your dad's not there.

It was always very hard to go see him and have to leave. I knew I wouldn't see him for a while. Now it's like, "Bye, later." Now that I'm older, I've accepted it, and it's no big deal now, but when I was younger, I used to hate it. I've been telling psychiatrists about it off and on since I was five.

Anne, 9 If I had three wishes, the first would be my parents never got divorced. Two, my parents would get back together, and three, that I'd get my own bedroom.

Riza, 18 I was about seven. Back then, when Dad was in town visiting me, we were discussing whether I still had the fantasy of the two of them ever getting back together. I said, "Well, sometimes I think about it, and then I think, 'Oh, it probably would just not turn out very well, so I think maybe it's not such a good idea.' " But I think about it every once in a while.

Carie, 15 I still don't really know why they got divorced. I mean, I know they had their differences, but they're still friends and stuff. It wasn't like a big goal in my life that they'd get back together, but I guess I've always hoped that they would.

Loretta, 21 I know the divorce was good for Mom, but it clearly isn't good for my brothers. Dad was always saying how he didn't leave earlier because of us, and I don't know how true that is. On the one hand, I know what they say, that parents shouldn't stay married for the kids. But I don't know. I guess they shouldn't 'cause if they're unhappy, then it's gonna fall apart at some point even if they try to stick around and try to stay together for the kids. Eventually it's gonna fall apart.

I mean, it was great for us when they were together. I can't say that it wasn't—even if it clearly wasn't great for them. They were unhappy with one another, but it was good for us. We had two parents who were there with us all the time, who we lived with.

Robin, 19 My brother said that my dad tried to get a divorce like three months after they got married, and they ended up being married for twenty-four years, so I think it's both their stupidity. I guess after they got married, Dad was just like, "Okay, you're not who I thought you were," but then he always tried to stick it out, and he thought it would fix itself. But if he'd left, then none of us would be here.

Roberta, 16 The divorce has helped me see that there are so many things out there. If they hadn't got divorced, then I wouldn't have met my stepdad, then I wouldn't have found out so much about the military, and then I wouldn't have gone to Turkey. I'm not saying you have to be divorced to broaden your horizons, but at the same time it makes you more aware. I learn so much more about people because I have four sets of grandparents, four different heritages. I've learned so much about personalities and characteristics than if I lived with the same two people my entire life.

Elliot, 11 Actually, I do think that they will get back together. But I wouldn't want them to get remarried. Or I would like that, but if they get married again, then they might get a divorce again, and then it starts it all over again. So I think they should just get back together, not married.

Barb, 18 I don't think it would have been better if they'd stayed together 'cause they would fight. I couldn't imagine how it would be like without them fighting because all I can remember is them fighting. I can't remember the years when things were peaceful because I was a baby. I do remember that my brother and I used to run to the door and greet Daddy and say, "Daddy's home. Daddy's home from work," and we were very excited about that.

Ken, 13 My parents get along like friends, pretty much. She was more mad before. She didn't like him as much when he drank. But now they're like really best friends. I think they're better now than when they were together. But I don't think they will ever get back together.

Just let it be like this. It's easier for me. The good part is not having two people gang up on you. It's just easier having one. It's like, if we got in a fight, it'd be easier one on one than two against one. You know, the odds are better for the person who's the smaller one. And that's me.

Nick, 17 I don't think I've ever really missed out on anything because my parents were divorced—maybe when Dad wasn't there for a soccer game, and things like that. When I was living with him, he was one of the T-ball coaches. He's just real interested in what I do, and he tries to do it, too. He seems to always wanna be involved.

Loretta, 21 Of all my friends here, none of their parents are divorced. I guess I have one friend whose parents are divorced, and I talk to her a lot, but all my other friends are so ignorant. I'm irritated by one friend who is still asking me, "Oh, your parents are talking? Do you think they're gonna get back together?" And that just isn't even a question in my mind. It's like, how many divorced people do get back together?

Marianne, 15 Do I wish my parents were still married? Oh, yeah, all the time. I still do that when I go to school and everyone's like, "Our parents are all married." Almost everyone that I hang out with, their parents are still married. Yeah, I definitely wish that they were still married. The holidays come, and I'm always so disappointed because I have such high expectations. It's this great, happy time that's gonna happen, and then I'm like, "What a disappointment," because I've built it up and built it up, and it feels like it'll never be any good again.

Heather, 6 I went to California for a week without my mom. I got to see seals and ride on Dad's motorcycle. Their house is so big, they should have someone else living there with them. My stepmother might have a baby. Maybe me and my mom should move in there, too.

The house is so big, we would all fit. Dad's rich so he could afford everybody.

Roberta, 16 My friends see their parents unhappily married, and they're trying to survive in this really gross, dysfunctional family, and I do not want my parents together like that. I do not need that stress in my life. The only reason some parents are together is the Catholic church frowns on divorce. I don't see why my parents got married in the first place, you know? So I wouldn't want them to be married now.

Wayne, 17 I wish they were still together, but I always think, "What if they were married and miserable?" Overall, I guess they're both happy. They're not partying, so that's good. The bad thing is I'm not with my father. I don't see him as much as I used to, so it has its pros and cons. But I guess as long as they're happy, I guess I'm happy. I mean, I'll always wonder, "What if?" But it's a part of life, you know?

Suggested Readings

Many authors have written extensively on the impact of divorce on children. Among the most famous in this area are *Surviving the Breakup: How Children and Parents Cope with Divorce* by Judith Wallerstein and Joan B. Kelly (New York: Basic Books, 1980) and *Second Chances: Men, Women, and Children a Decade After Divorce* by Judith Wallerstein and Sandra Blakeslee (New York: Ticknor & Fields, 1989). Both of these books are already classics in divorce research.

The following is a list of books that my colleagues at Marriage and Family Counseling Service and I have recommended to parents and children.

For Children

Banks, Ann. *When Your Parents Get a Divorce: A Kid's Journal* (a workbook). New York: Puffin, 1990.

Bonkowski, Sara. *Kids Are Non-Divorceable: A Workbook for Divorced Parents and Their Children.* Chicago: Buckley, 1987.

———*Teens Are Non-Divorceable: A Workbook for Divorced Parents and Their Children.* Chicago: ACTA, 1990.

Brown, Laurene K. and Marc Brown *Dinosaurs Divorce: A Guide for Changing Families.* Boston: Atlantic Monthly Press, 1986.

Gardner, Richard A. *The Boys and Girls Book About Divorce.* New York: Bantam, 1970.

Krementz, Jill. *How It Feels When Parents Divorce.* New York: Knopf, 1984.

Myers, Walter Dean. *Somewhere in the Darkness* (a novel for teens and up). New York: Scholastic, 1992.

About Children

Bienenfeld, Florence. *Helping Your Child Succeed After Divorce.*
Claremont, CA: Hunter, 1985.

DeSisto, Michael. *Decoding Your Teenager: How to Understand Each
Other During the Turbulent Years.* New York: Quill, 1991.

Faber, Adele, and Elaine Mazlish. *How to Talk So Kids Will Listen
and Listen So Kids Will Talk.* New York: Avon, 1980.

Gardner, Richard A. *The Parents Book About Divorce.* New York:
Bantam, 1991.

Hickey, Elizabeth, and Elizabeth Dalton. *Healing Hearts: Helping
Children and Adults Recover from Divorce.* Carson City, NV:
Gold Leaf, 1994.

Johnson, Laurene, and Georglyn Rosenfeld. *Divorced Kids: What
You Need to Know to Help Kids Survive a Divorce.* Nashville,
TN: Thomas Nelson, 1990.

Joslin, Karen Renshaw. *Positive Parenting from A to Z.* New York:
Fawcett Columbine, 1994.

Lansky, Vicki. *Vicki Lansky's Divorce Book for Parents: Helping Your
Children Cope with Divorce and Its Aftermath.* New York:
Signet, 1989.

Margolin, Sylvia. *Complete Group Counseling Program for Children of
Divorce: Ready-to-Use Plans and Materials for Small and Large
Groups, Grades 1–6* (for teachers). West Nyack, NY: Center
for Applied Research in Education, 1996.

Teyber, Edward. *Helping Your Children with Divorce.* New York:
Pocket, 1985.

Parenting Post-Divorce

Ahrons, Constance. *The Good Divorce: Keeping Your Family Together*

When Your Marriage Comes Apart. New York: HarperCollins, 1994.

Ahrons, Constance R., and Roy H. Rodgers. *Divorced Families: Meeting the Challenge of Divorce and Remarriage*. New York: Norton, 1987.

Blau, Melinda. *Families Apart: Ten Keys to Successful Co-Parenting*. New York: Putnam's Sons, 1993.

Cohen, William Galper. *Long-Distance Parenting*. New York: Signet, 1989.

Kaufman, Taube S. *The Combined Family: A Guide to Creating Successful Step-Relationships*. New York: Insight, 1993.

Kline, Kris, and Stephen Pew. *For the Sake of the Children: How to Share Your Children with Your Ex-Spouse in Spite of Your Anger*. Rocklin, CA: Prima, 1992.

Ricci, Isolina. *Mom's House, Dad's House: Making Shared Custody Work*. New York: Macmillan, 1980.

Ross, Julie A., and Judy Corcoran. *Joint Custody with a Jerk: Raising a Child with an Uncooperative Spouse*. New York: St. Martin's, 1996.

Thomas, Shirley *Parents Are Forever: A Step-by-Step Guide to Becoming Successful Co-Parents After Divorce*. Longmont, CO: Springboard, 1995.

Negotiation/Mediation

Fisher, Roger, William Ury, and Bruce Patton. *Getting to Yes: Negotiating an Agreement Without Giving In*. 2nd ed. New York: Penguin, 1991.

Kressel, Kenneth. *The Process of Divorce: How Professionals and Couples Negotiate Settlements*. New York: Basic Books, 1985.

O'Connor, Kevin E., and Frank C. Bucaro. *When All Else Fails: Finding Solutions to Your Most Persistent Management Problems.* Elgin, IL: Ritmar, 1992.

Ury, William. *Getting Past No: Negotiating Your Way from Confrontation to Cooperation.* New York: Bantam, 1991.

General

Beal, Edward W., and Gloria Hochman. *Adult Children of Divorce: Breaking the Cycle and Finding Fulfillment in Love, Marriage, and Family.* New York: Delacorte, 1991.

Gold, Lois. *Between Love and Hate: A Guide to Civilized Divorce.* New York: Plume, 1992

Gray, John. *Men Are from Mars, Women Are from Venus: A Practical Guide for Improving Communication and Getting What You Want in Your Relationships.* New York: HarperCollins, 1992.

Leman, Kevin. *Keeping Your Family Together When the World Is Falling Apart.* New York: Dell, 1992.

Acknowledgments

If it were not for my friend Jonathan Weinberg calling a decade ago to lure me away from Ravenswood Hospital, I doubt I would have ever entered the world of child-focused mediation. Once I joined the Marriage and Family Counseling Service mediation staff, Ruth Arkiss, my first supervisor, was crucial in helping me survive those early days in the trenches. I learned much from her, including volumes about talking with children who would rather be anywhere but in my office.

From the start I was lucky to join a mediation staff that was and is exceptionally professional, creative, knowledgeable, dedicated, ethical, caring, and talented. To be its clinical director has been an honor. To that end I thank Joan Massaquoi, my predecessor as clinical director, for pushing me into taking over upon her retirement and for recommending me for the position. I am also grateful to Judge Herman Knell and former domestic relations Presiding Judge Benjamin Mackoff for their support during that selection process.

Under my real name as well as a few noms de plume, I write regularly about music for several publications, including the *Chicago Tribune,* and I would like to thank my editors and former editors, Geoff Brown, Gary Dretzka, and Pat Kampert, for helping me to hone my skills.

The idea for this book developed quickly in a discussion with my wife, Karen Miller Royko, whom I thank as well, but if I listed all the things I should thank her for, these acknowledgments would stretch on for another hundred pages.

In refining my initial proposal for this book, I deeply appreciate the help received from Jan Lain, Tim Weigel, Stu Katz, and Penny Katz. Thanks for input into the embryo.

My father, Mike Royko, died suddenly several months before this book was finished. His advice was invaluable in moving me from simply having an idea to actually creating a book. Its completion is only one of many things I so wish he were still here to see.

Thanks to Sterling Lord and his band of Literistics, who patiently awaited the right publisher, and to Bob Asahina and Golden Books for being that publisher. Special thanks also go to my editor, Meredith Greene, whose accuracy and insights proved invaluable.

Several people helped to put me in touch with organizations and individuals that led me to many of the families whose tales appear in this book. Thank you to Kathleen Eggers, Dianne Elman, Rachel Seidman, Elizabeth Brachman, Maralyn Solarz, David Krantz, and my in-laws, Sherwood and Florence Miller. Florence has been asking, "When are you going to write a book?" since, I believe, my wedding day. Thanks for the nudging. And Sherwood, thank you also for the use of your office, which became my writing sanctuary during crunch time.

Thanks as well to Paula Kamen and her Transcription Professionals, Lisa Fuller, Jean Lotus, and Hilary Glazer, for the midnight-hour assistance that helped me almost make my deadline.

And most of all a huge thank-you to all the families who contributed directly to the content of this book, particularly the children I interviewed. I am truly blessed that each of you allowed me and the readers to enter your lives. In doing so you have enriched all of ours.

About the Author

Dr. David Royko has been clinical director of the Circuit Court of Cook County's internationally renowned Marriage and Family Counseling Service since 1994. He lives with his family in Chicago, Illinois.